Fables for Leaders

John Lubans

Fables for
Leaders

Illustrated by Béatrice Coron

2017

Place of publication:

Ezis Press
156 Front St. NE
Unit 700
Salem, OR, USA 97301-3459

Date of publication:
August 2017

First edition

ISBN 978-0-692-90955-3
LCCN 2017908783

Content

Introduction

In Ecclesiastes 12-12, Solomon said, "of making many bookes there is no end, and much studie is a wearinesse of the flesh." One might say the same about management and leadership books; "of the making of leadership books there is no end, and much study of these books is a weariness."

My hope is that this – yea, verily – yet another book on leadership will prove to be more boon than bane, that it alleviates more than aggravates.

There is, as readers know, an annual slew of scholarly and unscholarly leadership books. There are case studies of organizations and cultures from which we are to derive the "right stuff" for transfer to our own situations. Then there are the hagiographies and the ghostly autobiographical words of wisdom whispered (or shouted) down from moguls, all too many of the "Be like Mike" genre. And textbooks, not to be left out, are often more cut and paste and management by the numbers.

However, not to be totally dismissive, there are insightful works, helpful both in practical and philosophical ways, e.g., Robert E. Kelley, Douglas McGregor, and Mary Parker Follett's works among many others. And Elizabeth Samet's Leadership: Essential Writings by Our Greatest Thinkers is a perceptive anthology of creative writing on leadership.

Sometimes taking an indirect route, like fiction, may lead us to a concealed aspect of leadership, that "Eureka" moment that eludes us in power-pointed, bulleted, graph and chart formulations.

Consider this collection of fables and commentary an anti-textbook. Fables for Leaders has no acronyms to memorize, no lists of habits to acquire and certainly – for a management book – no quadrants and axes to retain.

Instead, these stories come from Aesop, 550 BC; Odo of Cheriton, 1200's; Laurentius Abstemius, early 1500s; LaFontaine, 1670's; and Sir Roger L'Estrange, 1690's; more recently, the Russian fabulist, Krylov, ca. 1810. And, I have included two original fables from a 2015 workshop, "Wisdom in a Thimble," which I led at the National Library of Latvia. I have written my own fables since 2011 and several are in this collection.

Fables for Leaders includes 100+ short stories of talking animals and trees…. and my ruminations on each. I emphasize the philosophical and ethical aspects in these stories – from across the centuries – to my own on-the-job experiences – successes and failures – and relate them to our contemporary behavior and decision-making.

We relate to stories, we remember stories, and these fable stories may help in thinking through and solving in untraditional ways, problems on the job.

This book gives you permission to take a break from the mechanics of management, to listen to Nature's wisdom. Let the wind whisper to you and hear what the moon's mother has to say. Fables can elevate us out of the mundane into another world where trees and animals impart wisdom or provide examples of guile and folly, gently guiding us in our search for values and behaviors.

I have long identified with the upside down and anarchic teachings of the Tao, which influenced post-Aesop fabulists. When teaching my class "The Democratic Workplace," I ask my students to consider the Taoist view (that which seeks to liberate the natural virtue within) as opposed to the more micromanaging practice of Confucian philosophy. The Taoist's world view is as much Theory Y as the Confucian's is Theory X. These philosophical notions I continue to explore and relate to the "unboss," a term I first used in my 2006 "Invisible Leader" study of a conductor-less orchestra.

"But, enough!" as Aesop might say.

Notably, Laura Gibbs -the pre-eminent scholar of the fable literary genre- has written 16 new translations for this collection.

Whimsical illustrations by international artist Béatrice Coron, capture the charm of this ancient literature and add to our comprehension and enjoyment.

A note on layout:

Each entry – in 7 chapters – sets forth the original fable (from one of the listed sources) followed by my commentary, an effort to draw the wisdom from these simple stories of lasting merit. I try to explain what the fable means for me, what memories it triggers, and, what applications I can make from the fable to my workplace experiences.

And, many fables feature a "My Thoughts" space to explore how this fable relates to you and your work. Use it; it is more than OK to write in this book, (unless you have borrowed it from a library).

I hope you will enjoy these fables as much as I do and that they will lead you to many unexpected and helpful personal insights about leading and following.

Now, for our first story!

Aesop

The Crab and the Fox

Crab once left the sea-shore and went and settled in a meadow some way inland, which looked very nice and green and seemed likely to be a good place to feed in. But a hungry Fox came along and spied the Crab and caught him. Just as he was going to be eaten up, the Crab said, 'This is just what I deserve; for I had no business to leave my natural home by the sea and settle here as though I belonged to the land.'

Moral: "Be content with your lot."

This disputable moral – aren't they all? – reminds me of the infamous "Lawsuit among the Adages." No, not cabbages, adages. You know, "Look before you leap" Vs. "He who hesitates is lost." The jury is still out.

In the workplace, one all too frequent refrain in opposition to change is the mantra: "If it ain't broke, don't fix it." We'll just keep on doing what we are doing, even if we are discontent. My injudicious response? "If it ain't broke, break it!"

While that sounds a bit too close to the insufferable certainty of Thomas Alva Edison's "Show me a thoroughly satisfied man – and I will show you a failure," I think judicious application of the "break it" principle might help untie those workplace Gordian knots that impede and frustrate.

Less dramatic but perhaps more germane is the Latvian folk saying about pursuing one's discontent for the best deal: "Why settle for a sandwich if you're invited to dinner?"

" If it ain't broken, break it.

Aesop

The Cat, the Cock, and the Young Mouse

Chapter 1
Us and them
Looks can be deceiving

 very young Mouse, who had never seen anything of the world, almost came to grief the very first time he ventured out. And this is the story he told his mother about his adventures.

'I was strolling along very peaceably when, just as I turned the corner into the next yard, I saw two strange creatures. One of them had a very kind and gracious look, but the other was the most fearful monster you can imagine. You should have seen him.'

'On top of his head and in front of his neck hung pieces of raw red meat. He walked about restlessly, tearing up the ground with his toes, and beating his arms savagely against his sides. The moment he caught sight of me he opened his pointed mouth as if to swallow me, and then he let out a piercing roar that frightened me almost to death.'…

'If it had not been for that terrible monster,' the Mouse went on, 'I should have made the acquaintance of the pretty creature, who looked so good and gentle. He had thick, velvety fur, a meek face, and a look that was very modest, though his eyes were bright and shining. As he looked at me he waved his fine long tail and smiled.'

'I am sure he was just about to speak to me when the monster I have told you about let out a screaming yell, and I ran for my life.'

'My son,' said the Mother Mouse, 'that gentle creature you saw was none other than the Cat. Under his kindly appearance, he bears a grudge against every one of us. The other was nothing but a bird who wouldn't harm you in the least. As for the Cat, he eats us. So be thankful, my child, that you escaped with your life, and, as long as you live, never judge people by their looks.'

Do not trust alone to outward appearances.

The anonymous translator – more likely accumulator since Aesop is easily "borrowed" without attribution – decided on this lengthy rendering, more like a short fairy tale. The precocious mouse's story advises caution when trusting someone, that all may not be as it seems. One rendering of this fable has Uncle Sam as the Predator Puss and guess who is the Friendly Fowl? Mr. Putin! Now, there's a reach!

So, remember sometimes even the best story can be taken and twisted to fit someone's unique, even disturbed, perspective. Are we really any less gullible than in the days of this fable, 550BC?

In the 80s, a young woman's father defected from the Soviet Union to America. Torn between her family in Latvia and her father in the USA, she nevertheless decided to join him. Surely, she thought, she would be immune to the effect of her exposure to the Soviet's daily anti-America propaganda. Still, when she got to NYC, she experienced a genuine, however irrational, fear – "a gun pointing at my neck" – that she would be shot on the street.

We should be mindful of the power of stories to shape, even distort, our personal views. Living in Riga, I've been told by some to never go to the Central Tirgus, the fabulous market. Why? Because bad people are there. And, I've been told with certitude to avoid one trolley bus route because I would be robbed. My real experience contradicts all these warnings. Had I followed this gossip I would be the poorer for it.

Aesop, a critical thinker, was forever peeling away the layers of untruth. He advocated in his own way, thinking that was "clear, rational, open-minded, and informed by evidence." Of course, we – in these enlightened times – are all "critical thinkers" are we not?

My Thoughts

❝ Even the best story can be taken and twisted to fit someone's unique, even disturbed, perspective.

Aesop

The Lion and the Shepherd

 Lion, roaming through a forest, trod upon a thorn. Soon afterward he came up to a Shepherd and fawned upon him, wagging his tail as if to say, 'I am a suppliant, and seek your aid.' The Shepherd boldly examined the beast, discovered the thorn, and placing his paw upon his lap, pulled it out; thus relieved of his pain, the Lion returned into the forest. Some time after, the Shepherd, being imprisoned on a false accusation, was condemned "to be cast to the Lions" as the punishment for his imputed crime. But when the Lion was released from his cage, he recognized the Shepherd as the man who healed him, and instead of attacking him, approached and placed his foot upon his lap. The King, as soon as he heard the tale, ordered the Lion to be set free again in the forest, and the Shepherd to be pardoned and restored to his friends.

One moralist has it: "When a man acts righteously, he can never be defeated by the punishments inflicted on him by his enemies."

Maybe. I'd say this story of the good shepherd shows how kindness can pay unexpected dividends. The shepherd, selflessly, helps

the lion, but he is not motivated by personal gain. He simply helps –
one being helping another. While the lion does pay back, acts of kindness are not Newton's Third Law about reciprocating actions. A reciprocated kindness is nice, but it cannot be anticipated. Our helping a
parent with a pram down a subway staircase likely has no reciprocal
action beyond a heartfelt thank you. Helping a man on crutches in
a drenching rain cross a busy intersection is kindness; the young
woman I saw doing this did so because she felt something, she knew
intuitively what to do – it is our innate Golden Rule, if we let it be.

My Thoughts

" Acts of kindness are not Newton's Third Law about reciprocating actions.

Aesop

The Cat and the Birds

Cat heard that the Birds in an aviary were ailing. So he got himself up as a doctor, and, taking with him a set of the instruments proper to his profession, presented himself at the door, and inquired after the health of the Birds. 'We shall do very well,' they replied, without letting him in, "when we've seen the last of you."

A villain may disguise himself, but he will not deceive the wise.

We all have them, those terrible, no good, very bad days. Even the ever-patient Aesop, ever ready to find deep meaning in the most humble of events, sometimes gets fed up and flips his lid (and finger) as a cartoon in the New Yorker magazine has it.

Regaining his composure, Aesop has these birds outwitting the cat. They're too savvy for Mr. Puss and bid him a less than fond farewell. And, so it can be in the workplace wherein we should be wisely vigilant for the bilker, the bamboozler, the puller of fast ones, and the flimflammer.

La Fontaine

The Dove and the Ant

 dove came to a brook to drink,
When, leaning o'er its crumbling brink,
An ant fell in, and vainly tried,
In this, to her, an ocean tide,
To reach the land; whereat the dove,
With every living thing in love,
Was prompt a spire of grass to throw her,
By which the ant regain'd the shore.
A barefoot scamp, both mean and sly,
Soon after chanced this dove to spy;
And, being arm'd with bow and arrow,
The hungry codger doubted not
The bird of Venus, in his pot,
Would make a soup before the morrow.
Just as his deadly bow he drew,
Our ant just bit his heel.
Roused by the villain's squeal,
The dove took timely hint, and flew
Far from the rascal's coop;--
And with her flew his soup.

A good friend commented wryly about staff having the freedom to help people regardless of the rules. But, in some organizations, he said "No good deed goes unpunished." Here the dove's good deed saves her life. In some organizations, nameless of course, there is another prevailing condition: "No bad deed goes unrewarded."

I think his meaning in no good deed going unpunished was in the context of a workplace in which a staff member goes out of her way to help someone; she may have to cross (horrors!) departmental lines or to take some extra time away from an assigned duty. And, in helping the client is then criticized by a supervisor for exceeding her authority. To those who say this is insubordination, a dereliction of duty, harrumph(!), etc., I would say, with an atrocious French accent, Au contraire, mon ami! Rather, this is doing what it takes to help the client and it should be what workers everywhere have the freedom to do. My apoplectic supervisor responds, "But what you blithely suggest could mean someone's deserting their station, or someone's spending precious time away from more important work! Worse, it is unfair to those clients we serve poorly. Oops, delete that!"

What was more important work for the dove? The truth be told, offering unstinting help to people in need, means a greatly expanding pool of clients who will not forget the favors done nor their source. If the staff member errs, that's not a world-ender. An apology will go a long way when the worker means to help not to harm.

And, overzealousness, as some might fear, will have its own restraint of time and energy and other work awaiting.

La Fontaine

The Lion and the Rat

o show to all your kindness, it beho(o)ves:
There's none so small but you his aid may need.
I quote two fables for this weighty creed,
Which either of them fully proves.
From underneath the sward
A rat, quite off his guard,
Popp'd out between a lion's paws.
The beast of royal bearing
Show'd what a lion was
The creature's life by sparing--
A kindness well repaid;
For, little as you would have thought
His majesty would ever need his aid,
It proved full soon
A precious boon.
Forth issuing from his forest glen,
T' explore the haunts of men,
In lion net his majesty was caught,
From which his strength and rage
Served not to disengage.
The rat ran up, with grateful glee,

Gnaw'd off a rope, and set him free.
By time and toil we sever
What strength and rage could never.

A variation on the preceding La Fontaine's Dove and the Ant; same message, good deeds are not always punished, often rewarded. Keep in mind the lion's munificence when someone at work or home would benefit from a helping hand. I've found an egalitarian spirit, like that practiced at Southwest Airlines, (see my book Leading from the Middle: "It's in the DNA: Infusing Organizational Values at Southwest.") SWAs core value of the Golden Rule can lead to productive ideas and unstinting effort (and results) from all, not just from those designated in charge.

My Thoughts

“ A core value like the Golden Rule can lead to productive ideas and unstinting effort (and results) from all.

Lubans

Canine Camaraderie

hey say a dog greets you each day like a long lost friend because she's forgotten, in the short term, seeing you yesterday. You're still in her long-term memory – of dog bone treats, balls thrown and fetched, long walks in rain or shine and shared moments of companionable silence – hence the effusive greeting: eyes sparkle, the tail helicopters as if lifting the rear off the ground, and her head ducks in stately bows. What joy!

I reciprocate and pound her side in heartfelt greeting, pull her ears and pat her head – a most convivial picture of man and best friend.

"Fawning!" you exclaim.

Nay, not forgetting.

A dog's never too busy or overcome by the daily grind or ruled by ambition to stop and greet you in the spirit of past camaraderie.

The moral: Our finest friend among the animals forgets us not, nor should we ignore those of our own kind we've met and liked along the way.

Lubans

The Traveler and the Leaf

 traveler in the mountains faced a challenge: crossing a chasm on a crumbling log. The chasm was too wide to leap over. Far below, water rushed over stones and boulders. While fearful of heights, the traveler knew he had no choice but to use the log, however rickety. Gathering his courage, he stood on the end of the log, hoping to find his balance. His legs trembled and faltered; this was not going well at all. He reached out to some nearby tree branches to steady himself. Surprisingly, as his fingers touched a cluster of leaves, he felt gently supported in the stillness, his balance leveled out. He gave a leaf a gentle tug but it did not give. He calmed down, took a deep breath and stepped along the log.

Later, as he ate by the fire, the traveler reflected on how he had been supported by a cluster of tremulous leaves, attached to a few flimsy twigs...

And so it is in the world, when a kind gesture, or a smile of encouragement, or a quite word of support – as seemingly insignificant as a leaf – helps someone meet and overcome an anxious moment.

My Thoughts

Chapter 2

Office politics

Aesop

The Fox and the Leopard

he Fox and the Leopard disputed which was the more beautiful of the two. The Leopard exhibited one by one the various spots which decorated his skin. But the Fox, interrupting him, said, "And how much more beautiful than you am I, who am decorated, not in body, but in mind."

A fine coat is not always an indication of an attractive mind.

Still, back in the day of martini lunches, wearing a jacket and tie (with pants, of course) would often get you a first class seat on an international flight.

My Thoughts

Aesop

The Farmer and the Snake

ne winter a Farmer found a Snake stiff and frozen with cold. He had compassion on it, and taking it up, placed it in his bosom. The Snake was quickly revived by the warmth, and resuming its natural instincts, bit its benefactor, inflicting on him a mortal wound. "Oh," cried the Farmer with his last breath, "I am rightly served for pitying a scoundrel."

"The greatest kindness will not bind the ungrateful."

This fable brings to mind a professional associate with a reptilian reputation. A predator at conventions, he would use his position as the head of a major public library to entice young professionals into "friendships" with promises of employment. Fortunately, his binge drinking usually precluded any reciprocation on the part of whomever he was soliciting. Whenever a newly made "friend" followed up on the job offer with a visit to this director's office, she or he would be met with a vacant stare and told to submit a resume to the personnel department.

Aesop

The Hunter and the Woodman

Hunter was searching in the forest for the tracks of a lion, and, catching sight presently of a Woodman engaged in felling a tree, he went up to him and asked him if he had noticed a lion's footprints anywhere about, or if he knew where his den was. The Woodman answered, "If you will come with me, I will show you the lion himself." The Hunter turned pale with fear, and his teeth chattered as he replied, "Oh, I'm not looking for the lion, thanks, but only for his tracks."

The illustrator Arthur Rackham imagined a resplendent wannabe hunter for this fable, fresh from a visit to the 1912 Abercrombie & Fitch. That's where the New Yorker went back then to get his elephant gun. In pith helmet, shooting jacket, jodhpurs and puttees, he'd be ready for big game. He was like many of us who sport Patagonia outdoor wear but have the good sense not to clamber up Mt. Everest without the requisite experience and support.

If clothes are words our hunter is well spoken. But, like at work, deeds count more than appearance. Confronted by lion-like change, we'll need courage and imagination more than a glib tongue or a Hermès tie.

Odo of Cheriton

The Weeping Man and the Birds*

ou need to beware of hypocritical politicians, as this fable shows. There was a man who used bird lime for catching birds, and the bird lime made his eyes water. As he was killing the birds he had caught, one of the birds remarked, "Look at that man! He is so good and pious." Another bird asked, "How can you tell?" And the first bird said, "Don't you see his tears? He is weeping with pity." A third bird chimed in, "And don't you see his wicked actions? A curse upon that man and his tears: he is weeping while he slaughters us."

So it is with the mighty men who go to church and pray and give money, weeping piously all the while. Yet they exploit and slaughter the poor and those less fortunate than themselves. The prayers and tears of men like that are an abomination.

Alice in Wonderland remarked after the Walrus and the Carpenter scarfed up all the little oysters: "(Of the two), I like the Walrus best," said Alice, "because you see he was a little sorry for the poor oysters."

* For a more literal translation, see in Sources, Jacobs Odo 15; see also Oxford Aesop 297.

Odo's story reminds me of a boss who fired a worker and then waxed solicitous about the ex-employee's well being. It was meant to come across as a most magnanimous gesture, shedding rays of empathy and (crocodile) tears upon the displaced and downsized!

It was, instead, all a scam, a persona cultivated for the environment in which this boss worked.

Some people regarded this boss as a kind person and an effective leader – indeed, he was foremost in volunteering to promote the institution, the quintessential "Yes man" to his boss. Like the first bird said, he was "so good and pious!" A few, especially those that were slaughtered by a boss "weeping with pity", penetrated the "good and pious" veneer and saw the magnanimity for what it was: a politically cultivated strategy for self-advancement.

My Thoughts

" Shedding rays of empathy and (crocodile) tears upon the displaced and the downsized.

Aesop

The Fox and the Crow

 Crow was sitting on a branch of a tree with a piece of cheese in her beak when a Fox observed her and set his wits to work to discover some way of getting the cheese. Coming and standing under the tree he looked up and said, 'What a noble bird I see above me! Her beauty is without equal, the hue of her plumage exquisite. If only her voice is as sweet as her looks are fair, she ought without doubt to be Queen of the Birds.' The Crow was hugely flattered by this, and just to show the Fox that she could sing she gave a loud caw. Down came the cheese, of course, and the Fox, snatching it up, said, "You have a voice, madam, I see: what you want is wits."

"Flattery will get you everywhere", sayeth the moralist. Or, as another Aesopist has it: "The flatterer lives at the expense of those who will listen to him." To add another twist to this classic fable, is for the crow to proclaim – fox-and-sour-grapes-like – that the cheese is moldy. But, that would be messing with this fable's simple truth. Consider the source of the praise. Can you trust the source? Might the praise be used to take away something you value? When I interviewed maestra conductor Simone Young, I asked her if she read her reviews – at the time she was riding a wave of popularity where she could not "put a foot wrong". "No." She explained: "If I read the good ones, I'd feel obligated to read the bad ones."

That's probably an effective way to keep praise in its place. She was not implying she was closed to feedback; she was just not going to be swayed by overly critical adulation or depreciation. She told me that, at the time, one of her most influential observers was her teen-age daughter. A thumbs up or down from that unvarnished source had meaning.

My Thoughts

Aesop

The Prophet

 wizard, sitting in the marketplace, was telling the fortunes of the passers-by when a person ran up in great haste, and announced to him that the doors of his house had been broken open and that all his goods were being stolen. He sighed heavily and hastened away as fast as he could run. A neighbor saw him running and said, "Oh! you fellow there! you say you can foretell the fortunes of others; how is it you did not foresee your own!"

This fable is a distant cousin to "do as I say, not as I do". I recall a consulting expert who could spout dozens of remedies to my shop's workflow problems. It was on a reciprocal visit to his place of business that I saw his workflow problems were even worse than mine. Apparently, while he had answers for me, he could not apply them in his own bailiwick. Now, I suspected that the problems were caused more by his untrusting attitude toward staff than with the mechanics of doing something. While he could talk about the mechanics with lighting speed, he never could relinquish control to the people doing the work. I had the good fortune to work with my staff, one on one, and the workflow improved, seemingly all on its own.

Odo of Cheriton

The Goat and the Ass*

his fable exposes those who have no respect for their superiors. There was once a goat who was the servant of an ass. The goat saw that the ass was simple-minded and unassuming, so he he decided to climb up on the ass and take a ride. The ass got angry and made himself fall over backwards, crushing the goat and killing him. The ass then got up off the ground and said, 'Just because your boss is an ass, don't assume you can ride him.' The same is true if you work for someone who is foolish or slow or old: be careful not to mock them, or else you might end up like the goat.

Well, I can identify with Odo's interpretation. I am sure there were times, because of my casual ways, I appeared simple and inept – and a few colleagues felt free to scorn and mock. I never did kick up my heels much about it, preferring to let my deeds speak. Because of my unassuming style, some folks saw that I was letting them lead, encouraging them to take initiative. I did not want to be ridden, I wanted to accomplish – with them alongside – what we set out to do. We did.

The mockers? Hard to say. Like the goat, a few got their comeuppance. Others, have done OK. Perhaps they are now the ass, un-deservedly scorned and mocked.

* For a more literal translation, see, in the Sources, Jacobs' Odo, "The He-Goat Who Wanted to Take a Ride."107.

Aesop

The Dog and the Lion*

here was once a dog who was chasing a lion as fast as he could, but then the lion turned around and roared at the dog. That changed the dog's mind, and he ran off with his tail between his legs. The fox saw what had happened and said to the dog, "You silly creature! You were chasing after someone whose voice was enough to terrify you."

Don't try to challenge someone more powerful than you are: you will fail in your pursuit, and you will be made fun of as well.

My daughter Mara's dog, Bridger, spent a year with us. She, Bridger, was probably a year old at the time. Since that year's adventures – which are described in my Leading from the Middle book – Bridger has matured and appears now to be a self-actualized dog, indeed an Apollonian canine.

Whenever she visits we go back to our daily routine. She reminds me when it is time for our early morning walk and when it is time for our afternoon walk. It's not much of a reminder, just enough of a presence, a nudging look at me or the door. And we're off.

* For a more literal translation, see, in the Sources, Laura Gibbs' Oxford Aesop 228.

In the early morning you'll see us, rain or shine, on a nearby forest trail. In the afternoon, it's a leisurely saunter around the block. One of the houses in the neighborhood has a couple small dogs and a cat or two. Usually I have Bridger off-leash because there is little foot traffic and because she is amazingly polite and well behaved, of course.

Not long ago, as we strolled past the house with the several pets, a high-strung barking erupted. Within seconds a tiny dog shot out of the driveway scrambling after Bridger. Bridger was un-impressed. Here was this 3 or 4-pounder, barking and snarling at a 50-pound black lab. "Bring it on," the little guy was shouting, "Bring it on!"

Bridger, imperturbable, ambled on. Then – Napoleonically thinking she was in retreat – he snapped at Bridger. Bridger spun around, opening her jaws about a foot wide, showing all of her teeth back to the molars. And, her hackles stood up three inches, adding another 20 pounds to her presence. The little dog, stunned, eyes bulging, ceased and desisted back into the safety of his yard. I like to think Bridger was a little amused.

The epimythium for my story: if you must bark, then bark at dogs your own size or smaller. And, in the workplace, if you insist on making asinine comments don't be surprised when a superior barks back, and then some.

" If you must bark, then bark at dogs your own size or smaller.

Aesop

The Goat and the Vine

Goat was straying in a vineyard, and began to browse on the tender shoots of a Vine which bore several fine bunches of grapes. "What have I done to you," said the Vine, "that you should harm me thus! Isn't there grass enough for you to feed on! All the same, even if you eat up every leaf I have, and leave me quite bare, I shall produce wine enough to pour over you when you are led to the altar to be sacrificed."

In the vengeful vein of "don't get mad, get even" the vine gets his own back.

In the office, I like to think, this fable might apply to the boss who is jealous of a star-follower's achievements – indeed that boss claims those achievements for herself while never publicly recognizing the worker's innovation and productivity. Turning about, the worker moves on and achieves recognition elsewhere.

And, this fable could apply to the goatish boss who claims responsibility for an organization's success but blames workers when things go downhill.

Aesop

The Sick Kite

 Kite, sick unto death, said to his mother: 'O Mother! do not mourn, but at once invoke the gods that my life may be prolonged.' She replied, "Alas! my son, which of the gods do you think will pity you? Is there one whom you have not outraged by filching from their very altars a part of the sacrifice offered up to them?"

We must make friends in prosperity if we would have their help in adversity.

The moralist appears to misconstrue the fable's meaning. Well, at least his take is not like mine. Even Aesop may have missed a beat here; the son's comeback ought to be, "But, mother, you taught me!"

Well, that's the nice thing about fables; there are as many interpretations as there are readers. I am reminded of my own situation as others are reminded of theirs.

For me, this fable seems more about alienating important people through outrageous behavior than it is about making friends in good times so they'll not abandon you in bad.

Of course, since kites are scavengers, the son was doing what he was meant to do. Kind of like those humans who believe they are destined to mandate (and more) to the rest of us where and how to live.

Aesop

The Plane Tree

wo Travellers, walking in the noonday sun, sought the shade of a wide spreading tree to rest. As they lay looking up among the pleasant leaves, they saw that it was a Plane Tree.

'How useless is the Plane!' said one of them. "It bears no fruit whatever, and only serves to litter the ground with leaves."

"Ungrateful creatures!" said a voice from the Plane Tree. "You lie here in my cooling shade, and yet you say I am useless! Thus ungratefully, O Jupiter, do men receive their blessings!"

Our best blessings are often the least appreciated.

And so it can be for those of us laboring in cubicle-land when we fail to support –nay, even undercut – the work of the folks in the back-room, be they one-door down or miles away. I've heard front office staff blame the processing people for delays and disruptions, when in reality the blame belonged much closer to home. In library-land, where I worked, some of the book selectors routinely explained to students and faculty that the hot, new books were not on library shelves because of the anal retentiveness of the processing staff. That made for a blame-shifting academic snort and chuckle.

The facts? We found that the processing workflows were hugely impacted by when a book selector ordered items. A few selectors delayed – for personal convenience – placing any new book orders until the end of the month and in some cases, until the end of the semester! Who's anal?

While we processed orders in one week – an industry "best blessing" – the selector-delayed orders impeded receipt of new books. In some cases, the books were already out-of-print, forcing us to go to used book markets, an extra step.

My Thoughts

Aesop

The Walnut Tree

walnut-tree, which grew by the roadside, bore every year a plentiful crop of nuts. Every one who passed by pelted Its branches with sticks and stones, in order to bring down the fruit, and the tree suffered severely. "It is hard," it cried, "that the very persons who enjoy my fruit should thus reward me with insults and blows."

Those flinging sticks and stones punish the good deed of the nut tree. So is the olive tree shaken violently by a machine to harvest its fruit.

But, only the truly unwise would do so much damage as to kill off the source of the harvest. Yet, we've been known to exhaust the land, to suck the rivers dry, to foul the air. Most of us know that we are here to husband Nature's resources, not destroy them. What we can do, each of us, is as obvious as consuming a cylindrical can of Pringles and tossing it into the street from your car. Take the lead – do the obvious – take care of the Earth. As for the trio abusing the nut tree, quote something from Chief Seattle. If they do not cease and desist, beat them with zest and relish.

Aesop

The Bees and the Beetles*

 he bees decided one day to invite the dung beetles to their home for a meal. The beetles agreed, and when they arrived, the bees offered them honey in the honeycomb to eat. The beetles only nibbled at the honeycomb, and then they flew away. To return the favor, the beetles invited the bees to dinner, and they heaped the table with platters of dung. The bees could not even eat so much as a bite, so they buzzed away back home. The dung beetles knew only carnal pleasures; the sweetness of the bees was beyond their comprehension.

Often Aesopian translators and editors added their own morals (or their take on the underlying meaning of each fable). Morals appear at the front, back and sometimes in the middle. Odo put his moral to this fable at the front, the promythium, the lesson before the fable: "Against people who enjoy only carnal pleasures."

Sometimes the morals appear to have little relationship to the story (like Odo's, above). One translator (Lloyd W. Daly) "defiantly titled" his translation: Aesop without Morals. (He relegated all the morals to an appendix).

* For a more literal translation, see in Sources, Laura Gibbs' Oxford Aesop 401.

If I were to put an apt moral to this story of bees and beetles, it would be that when we are confronted with a different culture we should still be polite and respectful. In this story, the dung beetles – lowly creatures when compared to the universally admired honeybee – exhibit better manners than the bees! Confronted with an exotic (for them) food, the dung beetles at least give it a try. The bees instead turn up their noses and buzz off!

Perhaps more relevant to the work place is the moral that we may value our contribution more than that of another unit, e.g. marketing over production. In fact both our contributions are important – indeed, essential. When we dismiss, criticize or ridicule the good faith efforts of other workers we poison the work place.

My Thoughts

Aesop

The Belly and the Members

he Members of the Body once rebelled against the Belly. "You," they said to the Belly, "live in luxury and sloth, and never do a stroke of work; while we not only have to do all the hard work there is to be done, but are actually your slaves and have to minister to all your wants. Now, we will do so no longer, and you can shift for yourself for the future." They were as good as their word, and left the Belly to starve. The result was just what might have been expected: the whole Body soon began to fail, and the Members and all shared in the general collapse. And then they saw too late how foolish they had been.

In short, the proverbial cutting off your nose to spite your face. And, so it goes when one part of an organization fails to recognize and appreciate the value of the other parts. There are libraries where departments do not speak to each other – it takes an emissary bearing a white flag to cross the line traced across the office floor in library glue and date due slips.

More notorious are university teaching departments in which faculty have not spoken to each other in 30 years, nor made a significant contribution to scholarship. Academic Deans dare not tread into this No Man's Land. A Provost might – with trepidation – knock on the departmental door, but why bother – no one's there. We are told intra-department communication (e.g. Who is going to teach those pesky freshmen?) is handled by the Swiss Embassy.

My Thoughts

66 It takes an emissary bearing a white flag to cross the line traced across the office floor in library glue and date due slips.

Lubans

Misplaced Pity

n a folly-filled freshman year at my Pennsylvania undergraduate college (Lebanon Valley College, by name) I went out for the football team; that's American football, the "smash mouth" variety. Why? Well a popular song from a bygone era sums it up: "You gotta be a football hero." The first drill for newbies like me was to block out another player. Now blocking is not tackling, but it is hitting the opposing player and impeding his movement, taking him out of the action. Ideally, you knock him off his feet. The player I was to block was about a foot shorter and 30 pounds less in weight than me. And, he looked kind of goofy. I felt sorry for the guy. We lined up and I took it easy. Big mistake. The little guy crashed into me like a mini bulldozer and knocked me flat. As I struggled up I wondered how many times he did that to larger players sappy enough to feel sorry for him. I wondered if looking goofy was a cultivated piece of his player persona!

So, play with respect for your opponent. Pitying someone on his or her appearance is disrespectful and puts you and your organization at a disadvantage.

Lubans

The Proud Blackberry

ne day a fox made much, in French, over July's first ripe blackberry. As usual, the berry was at the tip of the cluster, out ahead of all the others, yet green. The blackberry basked in Reynard's praise and remarked how proud he was to be the first, and such a magnificent first, shiny black, super sweet and juicy. The fox nodded and in a flash gobbled up the blackberry. The fox remarked, "Mon chérie, why do you take such pride in being the first. Have you not heard the tale of the tall poppy? For all his eminence, he's the first to be cut."

Therefore, don't be like the candle that brags on its flame only to see it put out.

A contrarian moral: On hearing the fox , a voice gurgled deep inside: "Au contraire, mon ami, my destiny is to be eaten and I have the honor to be the first of my brethren. You, Monsieur Reynard, are a mere vehicle, a bus d'auto. Next, when you hear the call of nature, I will fall onto the earth and soon reappear as a new cane to snag your raggedy tail with my thorns."

* An Australian term, it refers to an Australian's tendency to keep a low profile, to not stand out because, the tall poppy's the first to be cut!

Abstemius

Capons Fat and Lean

here were a great many Cramm'd Capons together in a Coop, some of 'em very Fair and Fat, and Others again did not thrive upon Feeding. The Fat Ones would be ever and anon making sport with the Lean, and calling them Starvelings; 'till in the End, the Cook was order'd to dress so many Capons for Supper, and to be sure to take the best in the Pen: When it came to that once, they that had most Flesh upon their Backs, wish'd they had had less, and 'twould have been better for 'em.

Prosperity makes People Proud, Fat, and Wanton; but when a Day of Reckoning comes, They are the First still that go to Pot.

So, unless you have friends at court, try like the dickens to avoid having the fattest salary, playing the cramm'd capon – however unintentional – at your organization, less you become a marked man among the envious and devious when the Day of Reckoning arrives. Wear camo; take benefits that do not appear in your salary line. Once the envious are in ascendance, they'll use your prominent salary against you and your job will be in jeopardy, regardless of past, current (or potential!) accomplishment. Like the Japanese say, "The nail that sticks up will be hammered down."

Odo of Cheriton

An Athenian*

f a man in ancient Athens claimed to be a philosopher, he had to pass a test: the Athenians would whip the man violently, and if he endured the whipping in silence, then they would declare him to be a true philosopher. There was once a man who presented himself for the test. The people whipped him, and as soon as the whipping stopped, but before judgment was passed, the man exclaimed, "I am exceedingly worthy of being called a philosopher!"

One of the Athenians then shook his head and said, "That might have been the case, if only you had kept your mouth shut and waited for our judgment."

I am reminded of the Polish folk saying "Broda nie czyni filozofa." ("If the beard were all, the goat might philosophize.") Obviously, the Athenians in this fable have a higher standard for their philosophers. There is something to the notion that if we hold steadfast and silent in the face of adversity, we are better able to say sincerely who we are and what we are about. It is like Mr. Stand-Fast in Bunyan's Pilgrim's Progress reaching deep into himself to resist the temptress, Madam Bubble.

* For a more literal translation, see in Sources, Jacobs, Odo 104.

Or, the moral of this story might be that any one, in declaring himself to be a great leader or great thinker or great writer, confirms the opposite. Often, such declarations of greatness are not explicit, rather implicit in a recounting of accomplishments, a process by which the teller self-leverages onto what he believes is a lofty pedestal.

My Thoughts

La Fontaine

The Horse and the Ass

n such a world, all men, of every grade,
Should each the other kindly aid;
For, if beneath misfortune's goad
A neighbour falls, on you will fall his load.

There jogg'd in company an ass and horse;
Nought but his harness did the last endorse;
The other bore a load that crush'd him down,
And begg'd the horse a little help to give,
Or otherwise he could not reach the town.
'This prayer,' said he, 'is civil, I believe;
One half this burden you would scarcely feel.'
The horse refused, flung up a scornful heel,
And saw his comrade die beneath the weight:--
And saw his wrong too late;
For on his own proud back
They put the ass's pack,
And over that, beside,
They put the ass's hide.

And so it is at work when we criticize colleagues in front of customers and others. It's easy, in cubicle land, to fall into this trap. If you are involved with the public, well then you appear to work wonders. Of course, your "magic" is only doing your job and thanks to a huge behind-the-scenes effort you are able to do it well. So – using an example from my field of work – when the professor goes on about how some things are hard to find in the library catalog or on the shelf, do you commiserate and tell him "It's those technologically challenged catalogers!" or do you shoulder part of the "burden" and find out what he is talking about and then share that information with your colleagues in cataloging?

Your rejecting any of the "burden" of something gone awry diminishes – like La Fontaine's haughty horse – you, the library and what it is trying to do. That gossipy professor won't forget your concurrence, tacit or otherwise. Probably, if properly primed, he'll spread the snide news far and wide, regardless if it be credible or not.

Similarly, when a department claims to be the ruby in the organization's tiara – all the while demeaning others at every turn – I am unwilling to share in the acclaim. The best teams speak not ill of their opponents nor should the best department speak ill of its counterparts. It is why in the list of characteristics of highly effective teams, I always include "interdependence". The best know full well they are part of a whole and do not stand alone – like some believe they do – radiating perfection over a landscape of mediocrity.

Lubans

The Pigeon and the Stone Lion

ong ago, when animals could talk, a pigeon grew accustomed to roosting on the head of a stone lion, something he would never have dared when the lion lived and breathed. The pigeon enjoyed strutting and preening on the lion's head for all to see, all the while mocking the now powerless "king of beasts".

Back then, not only could animals talk, but statues had resident spirits. The stone lion had one named Nemesis. Nemesis grew disgusted with the disrespectful ways of the pigeon and appealed to Zeus: "I was strong and honorable in life, why should this bird mock me and defecate on my head?" Zeus agreed and turned the stone lion into warm flesh and fur. The pigeon's next landing on the lion's mane was his last; the lion tossed his mighty head and snapped up the pigeon in his jaws.

Moral: Disrespect is no virtue. If you honor and respect something in life, don't begrime its memory.

In the workplace, I've seen pigeon-like besmirching of a former leader's good work, something that the denigrators would never have done to his face. And, sometimes, a good leader finds herself powerless, trapped between an unsupportive upper administration and a change resistant staff. Then, like the pigeon and the stone lion, the belittlers jeer with impunity. The moral of this story suggests, "Do so at your own risk; divine retribution might be on the horizon!"

My Thoughts

Lubans

Envy and Other Deadly workplace Sins. Kookaburra and Crow*

long time ago Kookaburra and Crow were friends. They lived in a land of perpetual night with little to eat. At Kookaburra's inspiration, they invited Sun to their dark and desolate land. Under Sun's warm rays, the land soon flourished. Crow and Kookaburra and the other animals learned new ways to grow and harvest food with plenty left over. No one was hungry and all were grateful to Kookaburra and Crow.

But Crow, a master of detail and cultivation, soon grew jealous of Kookaburra's greeting Sun each morning with his raucous laugh and basking in the glory of the dawn. One day while Kookaburra was away, Crow persuaded the animals to shun Kookaburra, saying that Kookaburra played all day and did nothing but laugh at Sun; anyone could bring the sunshine to their land. Many turned against Kookaburra.

Soon the land became dark and joyless – Sun no longer dawned, try as Crow would to Caw! Caw! a morning greeting. The animals began to fight among themselves. The few remaining crops dwindled in the pale light of the stars. Crow had secretly stored food, but would only share it with those who called him King.

* Inspired by the many Australian tribal stories.

Sun saw through Crow's treachery and followed Kookaburra to a new land, the land down under, where Kookaburra greets her every morning with hilarious and joyful laughter. In Crow's land, only a few animals remember the days of sunshine and plenty for all – it was like a dream, or so it seemed.

And we know why Sun never rises to Crow's, Caw! Caw!

Like Aesop's fables of old, my story has a moral, one that applies to the real world. It touches on how petty behavior, like Crow's jealousy, can lead us to lose something we value. To our chagrin, we can slip backwards away from the progress we have made. Crow's jealousy (and treachery) turns a sunshine filled world back into a dismal place.

My fable comes from my experience in the workplace. I have seen organizations give up solid and positive gains because of conflict among leaders; or, if we did not surrender our gains, I have seen businesses grow idle after achieving a plateau and incrementally slip back into the old ways.

Aesop

Father and Sons

certain man had several Sons who were always quarrelling with one another, and, try as he might, he could not get them to live together in harmony. So he determined to convince them of their folly by the following means. Bidding them fetch a bundle of sticks, he invited each in turn to break it across his knee. All tried and all failed: and then he undid the bundle, and handed them the sticks one by one, when they had no difficulty at all in breaking them. "There, my boys,' said he, "united you will be more than a match for your enemies: but if you quarrel and separate, your weakness will put you at the mercy of those who attack you."

Union is strength.

Well this fable might have a different outcome had Aesop known my story of "The Dog and the Stick" which follows.

Tik un tā ("anyway" in Latvian), so it can be in the world of work. When departments bicker, expect failure. Frank disagreements, spirited argument, respectfully presented, are not of which I speak. I mean a "backstabbing kind of love" – an aspiring country music writer's song title – the kind that uses a "perfumed dagger" – my first boss' phrase – and whispered gossip and nasty rumor that undercut one's own.

The only sure way to stop that is don't participate. A good friend has an effective way of dealing with someone who wants to engage in gossip; after a moment's pause, he changes the subject. He will not let the conversation degrade.

My Thoughts

Chapter 3
The organization

Aesop

The Kid and the Wolf

 kid standing on the roof of a house, out of harm's way, saw a Wolf passing by and immediately began to taunt and revile him. The Wolf, looking up, said, "Sirrah! I hear thee: yet it is not thou who mockest me, but the roof on which thou art standing."

Time and place often give the advantage to the weak over the strong.

Or, from another moralist:

"Do not say anything at any time that you would not say at all times."

In Oklahoma they say, "Don't let your alligator mouth overrun your canary tail." I learned pretty much to ignore the nay-saying and nit-picking of my proverbial "roof critics". Like the wolf, I knew who was doing the talking! Had these critics proof of their actions and achievements then I might have been impressed and taken notice. But, invariably, the loudest (and hollowest) mocking came from those with the weakest records.

Aesop

The Man and the Lion

Lion and a Man chanced to travel in company through the forest. They soon began to quarrel, for each of them boasted that he and his kind were far superior to the other both in strength and mind.

Now they reached a clearing in the forest and there stood a statue. It was a representation of Heracles in the act of tearing the jaws of the Nemean Lion.

"See," said the man, "that's how strong we are! The King of Beasts is like wax in our hands!"

"Ho!" laughed the Lion, "a Man made that statue. It would have been quite a different scene had a Lion made it!"

It all depends on the point of view, and who tells the story.

Indeed, there are two sides to most stories. Nor do we celebrate the times when the tables are turned and the lion scarfs up Bwana, the Great White Hunter. (A pretty monogram for your Abercrombie & Fitch Safari Jacket that, GWH, what?)

BTW, if you want to show Aesop's lion who's Bwana (boss), an unimpeachable source on the Internet reveals what you will need: "Any large caliber weapon with a well-placed shot, but I suggest a short knife for a REAL thrill."

Aesop

The Dog-Catcher and the Dog*

here was a man who wanted to catch a dog, so he threw the dog some food, and then some more food, but the dog wouldn't budge. "I'm not coming anywhere near you," the dog explained. "Your excessive generosity warns me to be on my guard."

If someone gives you extravagant gifts, they are probably trying to trick you.

The appended moral is largely common sense. Certainly, if a stranger stops his car and offers a young child candy, the child should say "No, thank you!" and scramble home to Ma and Pa.

However, morals tend to be absolute, kind of like Mark Twain's cat. The cat sat on a hot stove-lid and got burned. "She will never sit on a hot stove-lid again, and that is well; but she'll never sit down on a cold one any more."

I've encountered some of that in the workplace. I was a newly appointed manager, following on the heels of a departed micromanager. Things were not in good shape, so one of my first actions was to talk with staff and elicit their ideas. That's just the way I work; staff know

* For a more literal translation, see, in Sources, Laura Gibbs' Oxford Aesop 88.

what we need to do to get better. So, I asked. Some, like the dog in the fable, and the once-burned cat, clammed up, never volunteering ideas or suggestions. Apparently, their ideas had been repeatedly rejected – even ridiculed – by the former micromanager. A few of the staff gave me the benefit of the doubt, and more than a few ideas. A mutual respect and trust soon blossomed; they saw I applied the suggestion or told them to act on it. We improved, mightily.

My Thoughts

Aesop

The Travelers and
the Purse

wo men were traveling in company along the road when one of them picked up a well-filled purse.

"How lucky I am!" he said. "I have found a purse. Judging by its weight it must be full of gold."

"Do not say 'I have found a purse,'" said his companion. "Say rather "we have found a purse" and "how lucky we are." Travelers ought to share alike the fortunes or misfortunes of the road.'

"No, no," replied the other angrily. "I found it and I am going to keep it."

Just then they heard a shout of "Stop, thief!" and looking around, saw a mob of people armed with clubs coming down the road.

The man who had found the purse fell into a panic.

"We are lost if they find the purse on us," he cried.

"No, no," replied the other, "You would not say 'we' before, so now stick to your 'I'. Say 'I am lost.'"

We cannot expect any one to share our misfortunes unless we are willing to share our good fortune also.

OTJ (on the job), the unboss, never claims sole credit for organizational accomplishment nor blames others when things go bad. The unboss understands he is as much responsible for an organization's failure as he is responsible for its success. As a result, the salary multiple for the unboss is not 200 times the lowest paid worker; it's a much smaller multiple, permitting a greater share for everyone in the organization.

It should be noted that a prime factor in humankind's evolutionary survival is our widely distributed desire to cooperate and to be considerate of others. Aesop's selfish traveler comes up short on the cooperation gene.

My Thoughts

66 A prime factor in humankind's evolutionary survival is our widely distributed desire to cooperate and to be considerate of others.

Aesop

The Lion and the Three Bulls

hree Bulls for a long time pastured together. A Lion lay in ambush in the hope of making them his prey, but was afraid to attack them while they kept together. Having at last by guileful speeches succeeded in separating them, he attacked them without fear as they fed alone, and feasted on them one by one at his own leisure.

Union is strength.

One translation of this fable has the bulls quarreling amongst themselves, breaking apart, and falling prey to Mr. Lion. So, internal conflict – whatever the source can lead to disaster.

At work, I've been involved in my share of internecine strife – it's difficult to resist once you lose sight of the "big picture" and become part of a faction. I remember departments cold shouldering each other and panning ideas for improvement if made by the opposition, however worthy the ideas. We squandered work time and morale on disparaging each other. We gained little through the strife, but our customers came out worse. Internal jealousies that frustrate implementing good ideas and leave foolish policies in place only result in lower levels of customer service.

If you are a new leader/follower in an established and traditional organization (like the ones I've worked in) do you try to better understand someone's alternative view? That kind of openness could be like the sunshine and dispel the miasma of distrust, of disrespect. Or do you aggravate the gloom with the grey clouds of misunderstanding? Do you permit "guileful speeches" to go unchallenged? Do you get sucked into the bad-mouthing?

The only way out of a backstabbing culture is for the organization – initiated by a leader/follower – to practice mutual respect and trustworthiness.

My Thoughts

Aesop

The Blacksmiths and the Mouse

 mouse was carrying another mouse, dead of hunger, out of a blacksmith's shop. The smiths laughed when they saw him; and he, with tears in his eyes, exclaimed, "Alas, you men are so poor that you can't support even a mouse!"

The mouse gets one back on the jeering blacksmiths. The implied moral admonishes us not to laugh at others' suffering. That is a constant truth, but the mouse adds something more. He suggests that the blacksmiths are so cheap and so unproductive that they cannot keep a single, harmless wee mousie! Indeed, the blacksmiths' failings may have contributed to the mouse's demise.

And so it once was for me back in my 9-5 days. One supervisor took great delight in taunting me over the failure of a project. For him, it was a flawed idea, a bad process and deserved dismissal. I saw it differently, since I had had outstanding success when I applied the same project in my area of supervision. My critic, from the start, had resisted the necessary changes, never invested any of his resources, undercut the good efforts of others, and, frankly, came up short on the creativity index. So, his jeering served to underscore his failings more than any genuine flaw in the project.

Aesop

The Mule

ne morning a Mule, who had too much to eat and too little to do, began to think himself a very fine fellow indeed, and frisked about saying, "My father was undoubtedly a high-spirited horse and I take after him entirely." But very soon afterwards he was put into the harness and compelled to go a very long way with a heavy load behind him. At the end of the day, exhausted by his unusual exertions, he said dejectedly to himself, "I must have been mistaken about my father; he can only have been an ass after all."

And so it is at work when bragging and braying reveals an unflattering side of one's nature. Best to rein in our braggart-self on the good days since there's bound to be a bad day on the near horizon. Rather, tuck away the good times for reflection when the hay turns sour and the well water goes bad.

Take note of the circumspect farmer who knows better than to tempt fate. He never has a good year. At best, with barns bursting with bounty, he remarks, "Aye, it's a bit better than last year." Last year was a famine.

Aesop

The Wolf and his Shadow

 Wolf, who was roaming about on the plain when the sun was getting low in the sky, was much impressed by the size of his shadow, and said to himself, "I had no idea I was so big. Fancy my being afraid of a lion! Why, I, not he, ought to be King of the beasts"; and, heedless of danger, he strutted about as if there could be no doubt at all about it. Just then a lion sprang upon him and began to devour him. "Alas," he cried, "had I not lost sight of the facts, I shouldn't have been ruined by my fancies."

Arthur Rackham, one of the greatest and most prolific book illustrators of the 20th century, presented readers with a raffish wolf with a lupine leer at his lollapalooza of a shadow. Mr. Wolf is feeling mighty fine, 10 feet tall. "Ain't I somethin'?" just prior to the lion's lunge. And so it can be at work…

Lubans

The Snake and the Egg

ot long ago I got to care for a large horse, two outside cats, two chickens, one super Dog and assorted plantings and flowers. All went swimmingly until a serpent slithered into my Idyll. One of my chores was to feed and water the chickens. The chickens were in a portable, fenced-in coop. When I was done feeding and watering, I'd open the side door and pull out a freshly laid egg. A well-balanced free market, one could say. For their eggs the chickens got shelter, food and water and avoided the stew pot (and the passing fox or stray dog). And, in compensation, the farmer got the occasional egg or two for his breakfast.

Two days after I got to the farm, the egg production stopped; I concluded labor unrest about the new management – me. However, I did notice some stray feathers on the turf, apparent signs of a struggle, but the chickens were still there, uninjured and eating with gusto and relish the feed and vegetable scraps I gave them. So, I figured it was a critter, a snake likely, picking up some easy eating.

I never did see the perp, but I was told later that the culprit was a long, shiny, black snake.

And so it can be in the world of work. The "snake" – I know my bandying about the term is unfair to real snakes, a wrongly-maligned species – is anyone who steals another's person's work for personal, unearned gain. Plagiarism's the word. I recall a story I wrote reappeared with a few changes as someone else's work, now for sale at a term paper mill. Or, similarly, some idea I have shared freely is then picked up by someone and used without attribution. Use it to your heart's content, but do mention the source! It's simple courtesy as your mother will tell you.

Likewise, there's the leader who takes credit and fails to acknowledge the people actually doing the work. This boss never praises the person who thought up the great idea, who pulled off the impossible, who got the big job done. This organization has a single face – that of the boss, and you had better not forget it! Even worse on the corporate envy scale, is the boss who hates to hear public or private praise about the good work of a subordinate. One colleague particularly got a rise out of observing his boss when a visiting Pooh-Bah praised a subordinate in the jealous boss' presence. My colleague detected from the boss' expression a mental note-making to punish the person being praised; that there was soon going to be a getting-even moment. This same boss was, my colleague claimed, all about teamwork. Not exactly how most of us would understand it. He was all about anonymous teamwork for which he would then take full credit. Of course, if the team "failed" then individual team members would be singled out for punishment.

You want to know what happened to the snake? Let's just say egg production is back to former highs and the snake is now slinking around more ethereal pastures than heretofore; a solution not generally open to us in the workplace, at least not in most!

Lubans

The Raindrop and
the Snowflake

eus, the weather-maker, was listening with a growing impatience to an extended oration by the Snowflake. The Snowflake wanted a divine status in the weather pantheon; after all it was he, the Snowflake, who, in winter, transformed the brown earth and the naked trees into wondrous shapes and undulating landscapes. Why, he even capped Mount Olympus' awesome majesty with a white diamond crown! And, lest there be any doubt as to his superiority the Snowflake sniffed: "I cannot be compared to the Raindrop; that shapeless blob that falls to the earth and makes mud. Worse, the raindrop pelts down on my glistening snow and turns it into slush."

"Besides", the Snowflake unabashedly concluded, "I am unique; there's not another like me!"

Zeus rolled his eyes and turned to the Raindrop. "What do you have to say!" he growled. The Raindrop replied, "I am the rain, I beseech no special rank. I 'falleth alike upon the just and the unjust.' I ask only to be left in peace."

Zeus pondered. Then, he turned back to the Snowflake, "Yes, you are indeed unique. Unique as a grain of sand! While you blanket the naked earth, the Raindrop brings warm moisture and turns the earth green and fills the rivers and lakes. You, however, do mischief by covering the icy ground so Mankind slips and falls." After letting that sink in, Zeus roared, "That's my job, not yours, damn you!" With a couple blue lightning bolts he turned the Snowflake into what would become known as a "wintry mix" that was cursed by all. Neither snow nor rain but mostly an annoyance in its persistence to be something it was not.

And so it can be in the workplace when we employ prideful Specialists who sometimes lord it over the lowly "Generalist" and even our clients. Too often, when we require extra qualifications we exclude the outgoing and resourceful Generalist who will get the job done and win over clients. When credentials trump people skills – unstated, of course – we may be recruiting a wintry mix. If a new position involves collaborating with others – inside and outside the agency – then attitude (enthusiasm, energy, warmth, and natural intelligence) far outweighs a Specialist's unique expertise. Like someone – not Zeus – said, "Hire attitude, train for skills."

My Thoughts

Aesop

The Horse and the Goats*

ometimes you can see underlings who gossip about their boss; that is what this fable is about. There was once a horse who was being chased by a lion. Some goats saw the horse come running around the corner, and they made fun of him as he raced by, whereupon the horse replied, "You foolish creatures! You don't even realize who is chasing me. If you did, you would be even more scared than I am!"

Higher-ups are often mocked by their ignorant inferiors.

I'd add another moral, even though this fable already has two! "Before you criticize someone, walk a mile in their shoes." Until you do, you cannot fully appreciate what's driving someone else (Then criticize them. You'll be a mile away, and you'll have their shoes!). I recall an unpopular decision I made at work. It involved, as many unpopular decisions do, choosing the "best person" for a job. The departmental staff favored a person I did not believe capable, from

Laura Gibbs', the translator, notes: "In Caxton's telling of the fable, the story concerns 'thre lytyll hedgehogges / whiche mocked a grete hedgehogge / whiche fled byfore a wulf.'"

* For a more literal translation, see Sources, Laura Gibbs' Oxford Aesop 234.

past performance, of doing the job. So, I went with my choice, a less popular but, to me, more able manager.

At a subsequent staff meeting the matter came up. Just like the goats, the staff had a righteous good time jibing at me. Overtime, my choice proved to be the right one for the organization, but I suspect the critics still thought it wrong. On reflection, I'd make the decision less unilateral and more collaborative – I'd be less reliant on my "excellent qualities". Saying that, I understand that a collaborative decision might be far from what I believed initially – with urgent certainty – needed to be done.

Well, that's probably far afield from Aesop's fleeing horse and his goat critics – but that's where the story took me.

My Thoughts

Aesop

The Sow and the Wolf*

 sow, about to give birth to her piglets, was lying on the ground, groaning. A wolf ran up and offered to be her midwife. The sow realized that the wolf was only trying to trick her, so she said in reply, "The best way to help me is to keep your distance." If the sow had trusted that wolf, things would have been twice as bad: in addition to the pains of giving birth, she would have felt the pain of her own death.

An appended moral declares: "A man should be put to the test before you put your trust in him."

The sow knows intuitively not to trust the wolf. Humans are less transparent and may require vetting. In the workplace, I have had friends who have fallen away due to absence and distance or a lack of mutual interests. A very few have behaved like the wolf – "absconded", so to speak, "with the goods" and left me "holding the bag." All understandable to some extent – "it's bidness, just bidness" – but when it does happen there remains a debt unpaid.

When it comes to "testing" our relationships, the workplace rarely offers stark choices like between the wolfish and the lamb-like – it's

* For a more literal translation, see in Sources, Laura Gibbs' Oxford Aesop 311.

more complicated than that. Work relationships are more – forgive me – nuanced. Our wolves often dress in sheep's clothing or wear bow ties. But, there are clues, however tiny, for the observant. Does the new friend want you to join him in malevolent gossip? Does the new friend claim your ideas as hers?

My Thoughts

" Our wolves often dress in sheep's clothing or wear bow ties.

Aesop

Jupiter and the Two Sacks*

upiter, the ruler of gods and men, gives each person two sacks to carry. The first sack contains all your faults, and you wear that on your back. The second sack contains other people's faults, and that is the one that dangles in front of you, hanging around your neck.

As a result, you find it easy to see other people's faults, but you cannot see your own.

Re-reading this little bit of wisdom, I was reminded of one of the major mistakes – along with a multitude of inherent limitations – we are prone to make in performance appraisals, that of the "Fundamental Attribution Error." In brief, this happens because of our tendency to attribute favorable outcomes for ourselves as caused by our excellent internal qualities (fairness, hard work, perspicacity, etc.) while seeing our failures as caused by external forces (misfortune, envy, etc.) beyond our control.

However, when we view the outcomes of other people we use the opposite view – we tend to see the others' success as a product of luck and their failure as a reflection of their less than admirable qualities: incompetence, laziness or something else within their control. En Garde!

* For a more literal translation, see in Sources, Laura Gibbs' Oxford Aesop 527.

Krylov

The Musicians

he tricksy monkey, the goat, the ass, and bandy-legged Mishka, the bear, determined to play a quartet. They provided themselves with the necessary instruments — two fiddles, an alto, and a bass. Then they all settled down under a large tree, with the object of dazzling the world by their artistic performance. They fiddled away lustily for some time, but only succeeded in making a noise, and no more.

'Stop, my friends!' said the monkey, 'this will not do; our music does not sound as it ought. It is plain that we are in the wrong positions. You, Mishka, take your bass and face the alto; I will go opposite the second fiddle, Then we shall play altogether differently, so that the very hills and forests will dance.

So they changed places, and began over again. But they produced only discords, as before.

"Wait a moment!" exclaimed the ass; "I know what the matter is. We must get in a row, and then we shall play in tune."

The advice was acted upon. The four animals placed themselves in a straight line, and struck up once more.

The quarter was as unmusical as ever. Then they stopped again, and began squabbling and wrangling about the proper positions to be taken. It happened that a nightingale came flying by that way, attracted by their din. They begged the nightingale to solve their difficulty for them.

"Pray be so kind," they said, "as to stay a moment, so that we may get our quartet in order. We have music and we have instruments; only tell us how to place ourselves."

To which the nightingale replied:

"To be a musician, one must have a better ear and more intelligence than any of you. Place yourselves any way you like; it will make no difference. You will never become musicians."

You may have noted who's first violin (the erstwhile boss): the monkey!

In my business, we'd go through disruptive episodes; these were termed, euphemistically, "re-organizations". Unlike the candid nightingale, the participants in these administrative shuffles were reluctant to speak the truth, so we would re-arrange ourselves in hopes of some ineffable improvement in "communication" – our "music".

The telltale clue in most of these re-groupings was the lack of any objective measures to gauge the improvement. Did we sound better? Did we listen to each other to inform our music? Was our music sweeter post-reorganization? Did we interpret the score the way the composer meant it to be?

If anyone within the organization spoke up like the nightingale they'd be portrayed as overly harsh and too blunt, destroying the group's esteem and obstructing efforts to improve.

The re-grouping did have one positive aspect: the illusion that something was changing, somehow for the better.

On the other hand, I can say unlike Krylov's talentless and tone deaf quartet the Orpheus Chamber Orchestra – which plays famously without a conductor (a nightingale?) – does not hesitate to self-correct. In concert hall rehearsals, one or more musicians will go out into the middle of the hall, listen, and then report back as to the sound and ways to improve. I have long wondered if we in the workplace could not emulate this practice to improve our group efforts.

The nightingale, far from being a heartless critic, is what most organizations (and individuals) desperately need: someone to speak the truth.

My Thoughts

Aesop

The Grasshopper and the Owl

n owl, accustomed to feed at night and to sleep during the day, was greatly disturbed by the noise of a Grasshopper and earnestly besought her to stop chirping. The Grasshopper refused to desist, and chirped louder and louder the more the Owl entreated. When she saw that she could get no redress and that her words were despised, the Owl attacked the chatterer by a stratagem. "Since I cannot sleep," she said, "on account of your song which, believe me, is sweet as the lyre of Apollo, I shall indulge myself in drinking some nectar which Pallas lately gave me. If you do not dislike it, come to me and we will drink it together." The Grasshopper, who was thirsty, and pleased with the praise of her voice, eagerly flew up. The Owl came forth from her hollow, seized her, and put her to death.

This fable epitomizes how a leader's patience may wear out and dire consequences result. At the same time, there's a lesson about bewaring anyone who uses language like, "If you do not dislike", a certain give-away of double-dealing. But, then the owl, a reasonable creature, gives ample warning.

The fable raises the question, "When does the manager, the parent, the teacher discipline the insubordinate, the fractious, the obstreperous?"

At some point confrontation is the only option and there are life's lessons to be learned.

The grasshopper is a bit of a sad sack in Aesop. First he freezes and starves to death after fiddling away his summer and now he gets gobbled up by an annoyed owl. "Such is life" – the words uttered by Australian bushranger Ned Kelly at his hanging – might apply as well to our dearly departed grasshopper.

My Thoughts

Abstemius

A Hedge-Hog and a Snake

Snake was prevail'd upon in a Cold Winter, to take a Hedge-Hog into his Cell; but when he was once in, the Place was so narrow, that the Prickles of the Hedge-Hog were very troublesome to his Companion: so that the Snake told him, he must needs provide for himself somewhere else, for the Hole was not big enough to hold them both. Why then, says the Hedge-Hog, He that cannot Stay, shall do well to Go: But for my own part, I'm e'en Content where I am; and if You be not so too, y'are free to Remove.

Possession is Eleven Points of the Law.

The unwanted houseguest or the guest who overstays his welcome! We've all had them. P.G. Wodehouse tells, in a note on the oddities of American life, of an overnight guest who stayed for 15 years. Probably in Chillicothe, Ohio. For some reason Mr. Wodehouse, was taken with the name of this Buckeye town. But, I digress.

More relevantly, Grant Burningham's New Yorker piece, "Your Worst House Guest", documents dozens of outrageous tales of woe about hedgehog guests. There's a prevalent theme among the comments on these jeremiads: spineless hosts. If the hapless host showed some gumption and set limits the hedgehog guest would know the score and either get out or behave.

And, I suppose, that's the way it is in the workplace. Sometimes, when a worker behaves badly, the boss is to blame for making a poor hire and subsequently for not calling the behavior or for not adequately training the miscreant.

"It came seventeen years ago–and to this day

It has shown no intention of going away."

Edward Gorey, "The Doubtful Guest"

My Thoughts

Aesop

The Lion, the Bear, and the Fox

ust as a great Bear rushed to seize a stray kid, a Lion leaped from another direction upon the same prey. The two fought furiously for the prize until they had received so many wounds that both sank down unable to continue the battle.

Just then a Fox dashed up, and seizing the kid, made off with it as fast as he could go, while the Lion and the Bear looked on in helpless rage.

"How much better it would have been," they said, "to have shared in a friendly spirit."

Those who have all the toil do not always get the profit.

And so it can be at work. The research library where I worked was once in the running for a wealthy donor's gift. We thought we had the inside track. The potential donor had related, nostalgically, more than once, how when he was a poor farm boy the library had waived the rules and loaned him books. The library director's kindness started him on the road to success. He was now a millionaire many times over. The gift felt like a done deal; maybe enough money for a much needed new wing on the library or better a brand new library!

Lo, who should pop up as the cunning fox? None other than the dean of the business school who somehow got special dispensation to pitch his idea to the donor. The dean got the gift while the library got nothing.

Well, not exactly nothing. At the dedication of the business building named after him, the donor told the library story once again, about how wonderful the librarian had been and how he helped him on his way, a Horatio Alger story for these modern times!

Lubans

The Two Roosters

nce upon a time, a farmer and his wife were given a rooster, Rex by name. They added him to their brood of egg-laying hens.

Rex ruled the roost with an iron claw and a steel beak, brutalized the hens into submission; he'd strut and swagger around the barnyard, proclaiming with a strident cock-a-doodle-doo, that he was lord of all he surveyed, and ready to take on all comers. Spitefully, he'd take vicious pecks at bare feet and hands – even those that fed him.

Well, as we all know, those who rule by fear are often replaced by someone more ruthless, more ambitious, (petty tyrants take note) than the immediate tyrant.

One day, another rooster, likely fleeing a neighbor's stew pot, landed, literally, in Rex's yard. Bolder, younger and feistier, he soon vanquished Rex in combat and banished him to cower in a bush on the barnyard's periphery.

Left only with dreams of glories past, the lonely Rex looked around for a friendly face. He turned to the farmer and followed him about docilely. Alas, the farmer, while sympathetic with Rex's plight, knows Rex will soon have to meet his destiny – in the freezer.

What does this have to do with the workplace? Eventually, the office bully, the bad boss will be replaced by a badder boss or a more vicious bully, or, better, if the governing board displays some courage, will be removed for a true leader.

Rule by fear gets only temporary results and, overtime, merely mediocre. While hens may shiver at the tyrant and humans become wary, it's always at a cost to the organization. Low morale begets low production, low innovation and eventually a failed business, a failed organization, unless and until a supportive and compassionate leader – despising bully tactics – comes to the rescue.

My Thoughts

Aesop

The Hare and the Hound

 Hound started a Hare from his lair, but after a long run, gave up the chase. A goat-herd seeing him stop, mocked him, saying "The little one is the best runner of the two." The Hound replied, "You do not see the difference between us: I was only running for a dinner, but he for his life."

So, which is the more effective motivator: Fear or Hunger? In the fable, fear sends the hare flying; the dog's hunger will be placated at another time, probably at the backdoor of the cookhouse. Dinner can wait, one's life cannot.

OK, in the workplace what's the best approach for getting results? Kick 'em or trust 'em?

The martinet (overt or covert) boss can and will hurt you unless you produce. If well planted, the kick's an effective motivator, but what about in the long term? Can the boss keep kicking? What happens when the mistrustful boss leaves early or calls in sick?

Kurt Lewin tested three ways of leading – authoritarian, democratic and laissez-faire – and found that the democratic leader and his group fared best. Respect for and trust in a worker's abilities achieve more than disdain and mistrust.

Which leader are you?

Aesop

The Monkeys and Their Mother

he Monkey, it is said, has two young ones at each birth. The Mother fondles one and nurtures it with the greatest affection and care, but hates and neglects the other. It happened once that the young one which was caressed and loved was smothered by the too great affection of the Mother, while the despised one was nurtured and reared in spite of the neglect to which it was exposed.

The best intentions will not always ensure success.

Reading this fable, Johnny Cash's "Boy Named Sue" came to mind. As only Mr. Cash could sing it – premiered, no less, at San Quentin prison – it tells the tale of what it's like to be named Sue:

"I tell ya, life ain't easy for a boy named 'Sue.'"

Confronted at long last, Sue's no-good father congratulates himself:

"For the gravel in ya guts and the spit in ya eye

Cause I'm the son-of-a-bitch that named you 'Sue.'"

Maybe that's what Momma Monkey was trying to do, like Sue's dad, dish out some "tough love." Maybe.

Lubans

The Bear in the Tree

ot too long ago, a mother bear taught her newborn cubs to respect Nature and to share with lesser creatures. She taught them well. One cub, Ozols, excelled in his kindness and love of Nature, outdoing St. Francis of Assisi. But – there's always a but – his peers' love of Ozols (or Oz) caused a great envy in a wicked wizard living in the forest.

One day, Oz was gathering blackberries in the wizard's meadows. The wizard, in spite, (remember he was wicked and a narcissist) turned Ozols into a tree.

Everyone wondered where Oz was. Then one day, a tiny bird, a wren, landed on a tree in the forest and was surprised to see a familiar face.

"Is that you, Oz?"

"Yes, it is me", whispered the tree. The wren, happy, let loose a liquid, rolling whistle that resonated throughout the forest.

"The wizard did this. Can you help?" asked the trapped Oz.

The little bird, remembering Oz's kindness, simply said, "Of course."

Now, you might be wondering how could a tiny bird do anything? He knew to ask others for help. Soon, a mighty number of the wren family gathered to hear the news about Ozols. That night they flew to the wizard's hunting lodge and, in concert, began to sing, jerking the Wizard out of his warm and cozy bed. Outraged, he tore open the front door but saw no one – short-sighted, he refused vainly to wear glasses and it was pitch-dark. He slammed the door and went back in, hiding his head under a pillow. The wrens started in again; the noise from a dozen different wren songs was a deafening cacophony and went on all night. The next night and the next the wrens came back. The wizard could not sleep – and with dark circles under his blood-shot eyes, finally gave in, pleading, "What do you want?"

"Free Oz!", the little bird demanded.

And so, Ozols was a bear again – free to live his life in the forest. The wizard? Well he'd learned if he was to get any sleep, he'd better quit being such a jerk.

Aesop

The Crow and the Pitcher

Crow perishing with thirst saw a pitcher, and hoping to find water, flew to it with delight. When he reached it, he discovered to his grief that it contained so little water that he could not possibly get at it. He tried everything he could think of to reach the water, but all his efforts were in vain. At last he collected as many stones as he could carry and dropped them one by one with his beak into the pitcher, until he brought the water within his reach and thus saved his life.

Necessity is the mother of invention.

On the job, when we had a problem to solve and the only apparent option was to spend more to do the same thing, I would ask a few questions: What would happen if we stopped doing this? What could we do instead? How does this add value for our clients? And, finally, What do you (the people with the problem) recommend we do?

No, I was not being the bully-boss putting out inane questions. My questions were meant to trigger a creative response – to create urgency, a necessity, like Aesop's crow encountered, to get us out of the rut of incremental thinking. The crow's ingenuity, pushed by necessity, saves his life. It was my intent to prompt insightful thinking, to consider alternatives and options, like what can we substitute, combine, modify, or, yes, eliminate? I know some staff were figuratively shaking their heads and thinking: "There simply are no other ways to do this. If only you knew why we do what we do, then you would not ask these silly questions!" Unlike the crow, they'd willingly go thirsty.

Creative and resourceful staff, when given the opportunity to pause and reflect, often will find a way. And, overtime, the best staff won't need any prompting; they'll let you know what they've come up with and implemented! Yes, with freedom at work comes a mutual responsibility: for the boss to let go and for those doing the work to make decisions about how to do that work.

My Thoughts

Lubans

The Three Villages

ong ago, in a far away land, two trolls enthralled six villages, each tyrannizing three. The trolls were feared far and wide; their foul breath and heavy, hairy hands seemed everywhere. Each year the villagers had to give half of their earnings and crops to the trolls. The trolls grew rich and the people grew poor. The villagers suffered in silence.

One of the trolls died – he fell off a bridge – some say he jumped, others that he was pushed. Regardless, the people reclaimed those three villages but the other troll, albeit growing old and feeble, tightened his grip on his three.

The enslaved villagers whispered of freedom, about reclaiming what was rightfully theirs. But how to do this! The troll permitted only one festival, an annual gathering: the summer solstice. The crops were planted and well underway; soon he would get his half share. And, the days were long, so why not let the peasants have a party, as long as they paid for it, fed his minions and went back to the fields the next day. By mid-night the troll's mercenaries were in a stupor from a surfeit of freshly baked bread, summer cheese and gallons of beer and more gallons of beer.

While the troll's minions blissfully snored, the villagers met at the bon fire and spoke of freedom, but none knew of a way to rid the land of the troll. The children listened, fidgeted; then, the village Innocent – a shy young man who was known to say the unexpected – spoke up: "Let's beguile the troll with a chain of people, holding hands stretching across our three villages. He will see us united as one." After thrashing it out, the villagers championed the idea: "The troll will be befuddled and know not what to do." "Yet, others will know; our neighbors will know, and the people in the free villages will know and they will help." "And, besides the troll is old and rickety; maybe he will give it up," some wished.

So, all the villagers agreed to hold hands the next day in a chain that stretched along the dirt road, across the bridges and along the lake and through the forest, across the farmlands. Morning came and slowly people gathered, coming down the lanes, through the forests, along the pastures, some dressed in their colorful folk clothes – the ones forbidden by the troll, so this was a risk, but the mercenaries snored on. Soon the chain ran through the three villages and when the neighboring villages heard about it, they too linked hands and created a chain from their villages to those of the troll. They stood and sang and remembered how life was before the troll, how they farmed the land, built their barns, raised bees, made cheese and beer, and baked bread and danced and sang their songs.

The troll awakened to the forbidden music and peered out of his castle window. He was enraged by what he saw but knew not what to make of it – a long line of old and young people, babies in arms, children, even dogs and cats as far as his eye could see in each direction.

He roared, demanded they disband, or be punished. He stomped out of the castle and glared at the villagers from an arched bridge; he fumed and frowned at the crowd. No one moved. He then called for his minions to separate the people, to tear them apart and throw them into the ditches, but no mercenaries appeared – they were still sound asleep. In a temper tantrum, he stomped his feet, clenched his massive fists and jumped up and down. The floorboards gave and he crashed through (like Rumplestiltskin) and plummeted into the rushing river, never to be seen again.*

And, that is how a peaceful linking of hands across those three villages rid them of the troll and freedom was regained.

And, so it was on August 23, 1989 two million people linked hands across the lands of Estonia, Latvia, and Lithuania – "The Baltic Way" (Baltijas ceļš).

This human line 600 kilometers (373 miles) in length ran through capital cities, forests, along lakes and rivers, across bridges and national borders. The people flew forbidden national flags and sang forbidden national anthems and stood connected and called attention to the secret and brutal fraud perpetrated by Hitler and Stalin in 1941 and perpetuated by the Soviet Union.

On March 11, 1990 the independence of the Republic of Lithuania was officially restored and in the following year Latvia and Estonia were free once again.

* Some say the troll can be heard every August 23rd, grumbling and cursing under that bridge. Will you cross that bridge?

My Thoughts

Lubans

The Beech Tree in Winter

The organization

Loyalty

ow listen well and I will tell you why the Beech keeps its leaves in winter. Long ago all the trees flourished and grew many feet into the sky, as high as they could go. Then a drought came and the trees began to suffer. Their leader, the Great Oak, called a council of trees to consider what to do. This was a time when trees could walk and talk. Many in the assembly thought it best to leave for elsewhere; certainly, over the mountains there must be rain and rich dirt! A few blamed the Great Oak for the hardship – it was a matter of poor leadership, indeed failed leadership! some harrumphed. Yes, trees back then could do that just like people.

Many trees joined in the criticism, and advised – with much rustling and creaking of branches – crossing the mountains. The Oak heard, but said he was staying. It was best, in his eyes, to stand silently and wait in wisdom: use less food from the earth and produce less fruit, and wait for the rains. All, including their animal friends, will have to do with less.

The Beech Tree listened and considered. She remembered Grandmother Beech's stories about the joy of bountiful days and the misery of lean times. "There will be times of plenty, there will be times of less. Some years there will be little growth, other years will be full of new leaves and heavy hanging fruit. Never is each year the same." She taught that only patience and sacrifice will get a tree through a bad year on into a good one.

Then, the Beech Tree spoke up and said she would stay by the side of Great Oak.

Hearing Beech Tree's wisdom, many trees reconsidered and stayed. Some trees did pick up their roots and move away, seeking a gentler climate. They found little improvement – the drought was throughout the land on both sides of the mountain range. Their energy spent on crossing the mountains, many died.

Those that stayed with the Great Oak suffered but survived.

Eventually, the rains came and the forest turned green once again. At the next council, the Great Oak told all the trees that the Beech Tree would keep its autumn leaves through the winter. It was to remind everyone of the importance of loyalty, faith, and patience – and of Beech's independence. Her leaves would shine brightly in bands of gold amidst winter's grey. "Those un-fallen leaves will remind us of the warm rain and sun, the gentle winds, and our soon-to-return animal friends, small and large and winged."

My Thoughts

Chapter 4
Problems

Aesop

The Fisherman and His Nets

 Fisherman, engaged in his calling, made a very successful cast and captured a great haul of fish. He managed by a skillful handling of his net to retain all the large fish and to draw them to the shore; but he could not prevent the smaller fish from falling back through the meshes of the net into the sea.

For so brief a fable, it's a puzzler. Is it about the failings of the net – a design issue – or is it about "big fish" vs. "little fish"? About the wisdom of staying small and un-noticed vs. becoming large and prominent to the "fisherman"? The former lives for another day while the latter dies.

What is the "net"? Something to be avoided; certainly when entrapped, it's largely over. Or is the "net" destiny and impossible to avoid?

One could conclude that not speaking up in the workplace is a smart career strategy. Abraham Lincoln's humorous words come to mind, "Better to remain silent and be thought a fool than to speak out and remove all doubt." (Alas, those are words I should have heeded more often than I did.)

Yet, Mr. Lincoln spoke out, freeing the enslaved (at a great cost). Should he instead have remained silent and let things work themselves out?

Sometimes, try as we might to remain a small fish, to go un-noticed, we have to choose between what we believe is right or wrong.

Aesop

The Dogs and the Crocodiles*

n ancient legend says that dogs who drank from the Nile had to do so on the run in order to escape the crocodiles. One day, a crocodile tried to trick a dog as he ran along the water's edge, taking little sips. "My dear dog," the crocodile said, "drink as much as you want; no need to hurry, no need to be afraid." The dog replied, "You can't fool me, crocodile! I might be tempted to stop and drink my fill, but I know you are waiting to gobble me up."

Lesson learned: Don't waste your time with someone who is wise to you and your tricks; you'll be the one who ends up a fool.

After a night of rain, Bridger (a black lab) and I would do our usual walk, off leash, on the forest trail. There'd be long puddles and Bridger, in a run, would skim them, her mouth agape, savoring the water. If we were in a low and swampy area, I'd admonish her to not drink, "It's bad, it's probably got sewage in it!" She'd give me a baleful look over her black shoulder and keep right on. Now I know what that look meant: "Man, don't you know? I'm looking out for the crocs!"

* For a more literal translation, see Sources, Laura Gibbs' Oxford Aesop 102.

Parentally, Thomas Bewick cautions us: "It is ever dangerous to be long conversant with persons of bad character." So, when you are next strolling by the "Nile" or other hot spot on Miami's South Beach, beware the crocs hangin' outside lest you metamorphosize into an ass.

My Thoughts

La Fontaine

The Cat and the Fox

he Cat and the Fox once took a walk together,
Sharpening their wits with talk about the weather
And as their walking sharpened appetite, too,
They also took some things they had no right to.
Cream, that is so delicious when it thickens,
Pleased the Cat best. The Fox liked little chickens.

With stomachs filled, they presently grew prouder,
And each began to try to talk the louder--
Bragging about his skill, and strength, and cunning.
"Pooh!" said the Fox. "You ought to see me running.
Besides, I have a hundred tricks. You Cat, you!
What can you do when Mr. Dog comes at you!"
"To tell the truth," the Cat said, "though it grieve me
I've but one trick. Yet that's enough--believe me!"

There came a pack of fox-hounds--yelping, baying.
"Pardon me", said the Cat. "I can't be staying.
This is my trick." And up a tree he scurried,
Leaving the Fox below a trifle worried.

In vain he tried his hundred tricks and ruses
(The sort of thing that Mr. Dog confuses)--
Doubling, and seeking one hole, then another--
Smoked out of each until he thought he'd smother.
At last as he once more came out of cover,
Two nimble dogs pounced on him--All was over!

"Common sense is always worth more than cunning" is how one moralist put it.

Or, as Occam had it: "When you hear hoof beats, think horses not zebras." The simple answer to a problem is often the best answer. Tell that to my adminstrative contemporaries for whom complexity trumped simplicity. They never believed the corollary that simple is difficult, complex is easy. For them, a simple solution always improved by adding a few curlicues here and there. More important is understanding the problem. The cat understands and survives. The fox, offers up his 100 ruses and dies.

Abstemius

Wax and Brick

here was a Question started once about Wax and Brick, why the one should be so brittle, and liable to be broken with every Knock, and the other bear up against all Injuries and Weathers, so durable and firm. The Wax philosophiz'd upon the Matter, and finding out at last, that it was Burning made the Brick so hard, cast itself into the Fire, upon an Opinion that Heat would harden the Wax too; but that which Consolidated the one, Dissolv'd the other."

'Tis a Folly to try Conclusions, without understanding the Nature of the Matter in Question.

The wax candle illustrates the mistakes we make when we leap to answers – conclusions – rather than stop and define what the problem – question – really is. Coming up with a solution is easy once you have successfully defined the problem.

H. L. Mencken is credited with this insight:

"For every complex problem there is an answer that is clear, simple, and wrong."

A personal example, I was in a two-person canoe (me in the bow and my friend in the stern) and we were in swift white water. Coming up were a series of boulders, large enough to damage boats and boaters.

We angled around one or two and then – our skills far from Olympic – the water pushed us sideways toward another boulder. Both of us leaned AWAY from the oncoming rock – natural and intuitive, but wrong. Leaning away, tips the boat into the rushing water. Leaning towards the rock, as instructed, would tilt the side of the canoe out of the water and we'd be able to use our paddles to steer around the rock. Instead, the water rushed over the lowered gunwale – sinking the canoe and making us about as navigable as a brick underwater. In a few seconds the force of the rushing water "wrapped" our underwater canoe around the rock – immobilizing it – and we had to be rescued.

My Thoughts

Aesop

The Man and the Satyr

Man and a Satyr became friends, and determined to live together. All went well for a while, until one day in winter-time the Satyr saw the Man blowing on his hands. 'Why do you do that!' he asked. "To warm my hands," said the Man. That same day, when they sat down to supper together, they each had a steaming hot bowl of porridge, and the Man raised his bowl to his mouth and blew on it. "Why do you do that!" asked the Satyr. "To cool my porridge," said the Man. The Satyr got up from the table. "Good-bye," said he, "I'm going: I can't be friends with a man who blows hot and cold with the same breath."

Isn't this just how some friendships come to an end, over some inane misunderstanding? The man "blows hot and cold", so the satyr abandons the friendship. Why does he not accept that the same action might be the result of two different causes?

A long time friend of mine ceased being a friend. Why, I have no reason. Was it me or was it a series of things that resulted in his turning away?

Maybe the man in the fable should have said to the satyr something like, "Are you serious? You want to quit being friends because I blow on my hands and on my soup, an easily explainable behavior?"

May not make any difference, but worth a try.

Aesop

The Crow and the Serpent

Crow in great want of food saw a Serpent asleep in a sunny nook, and flying down, greedily seized him. The Serpent, turning about, bit the Crow with a mortal wound. In the agony of death, the bird exclaimed: "O unhappy me! who have found in that which I deemed a happy windfall the source of my destruction."

And, so it can be at work. Sometimes, in haste, what we think is the best solution turns out to be the worst. The difficulty for the manager is knowing when to "leap" on a solution and when to "look" and think twice. In an organization of "yes people", accommodators, and compromisers, the lack of spirited disagreement can lead to poor choices.

Aesop

The Wasp and the Snake

 wasp seated himself upon the head of a Snake and, striking him unceasingly with his stings, wounded him to death. The Snake, being in great torment and not knowing how to rid himself of his enemy, saw a wagon heavily laden with wood, and went and purposely placed his head under the wheels, saying, "At least my enemy and I shall perish together."

Dying with your enemy seems extreme; is there not an alternative step to avoid this Lose/Lose outcome?

Since Aesop's animals can talk, the snake should find out what's bugging the wasp, what is the source of the conflict? It's doubtful the wasp is after the snake as food – there's some other reason for it to afflict so much suffering on a fellow creature. So, identify the grievance. If some concession or compromise can be made, then make it. Alternatively, instead of the snake crawling into traffic he could look for water, dive in and be rid of the wasp.

Now that's all easily said. Advice giving is vastly different from advice taking! I worked in an academic setting for many years. Among the faculty there were legendary feuds, some never resolved until the death or departure of the combatants – indeed, they died with their enemy. And, I've seen departmental faculty who do not talk to each other, ever, because of some philosophical difference. Not exactly dying with your enemy, more a mutual suffering (dogs in the manager). And, I've seen the two enemy camps waste creative effort in trying to enlist support through complaining ad naseum to any one trapped into listening. Many organizations but the most blessed have their own versions of petty, hardly irreconcilable, conflict. Those spiteful jealousies and lack of trust are detrimental to the institution. Our service and production suffer, decisions are avoided or delayed, and resources are not well used. Nor are customers as well served as they might be.

So, to take my advice for the snake and the wasp, why, in my time, did we not address it? Why did I not approach the opposition and open the discussion about what's going on and how can we get past it? I think it would have been easy to do, if only we had done it!

My Thoughts

Aesop

The Ass and His Driver

n Ass, being driven along a high road, suddenly started off and bolted to the brink of a deep precipice. While he was in the act of throwing himself over, his owner seized him by the tail, endeavoring to pull him back. When the Ass persisted in his effort, the man let him go and said, "Conquer, but conquer to your cost."

Or, as another moralist bluntly puts it: "The fable criticizes people who are destroyed by their own stupidity."

Who's the stupid? The donkey? The raging driver? I initially thought it was the donkey, but I think Aesop's epimythium (the moral at the end of the fable) is likely referring to the driver's behavior. Instead of pushing the donkey over the cliff, the driver should be doing everything to save the donkey. Maybe pull out a bit of sugar, a carrot, whatever to distract the donkey from his self-destruction. After all the donkey is the driver's livelihood; it's unlikely the driver has a back-up at home.

And so it goes on the job. We may have a fellow worker who seems hell-bent on getting fired. Should we ignore the behavior or should we, with a kind word or two, try to divert the person from going over the cliff?

La Fontaine

The Two Bulls And The Frog

wo bulls engaged in shocking battle,
Both for a certain heifer's sake,
And lordship over certain cattle,
A frog began to groan and quake.
"But what is this to you?"
Inquired another of the croaking crew.
"Why, sister, don't you see,
The end of this will be,
That one of these big brutes will yield,
And then be exiled from the field?
No more permitted on the grass to feed,
He'll forage through our marsh, on rush and reed;
And while he eats or chews the cud,
Will trample on us in the mud.
Alas! to think how frogs must suffer
By means of this proud lady heifer!"
This fear was not without good sense.
One bull was beat, and much to their expense;
For, quick retreating to their reedy bower,
He trod on twenty of them in an hour.

Of little folks it oft has been the fate
To suffer for the follies of the great.

Yea, verily. In my business I'd see "perfumed dagger" stuff, like my first boss used to say, in the administrative suite akin to the bulls battling over a pasture. The loser would get "kicked upstairs", ousted from a position of some importance and "promoted" to another of an apparently higher status but far less influential. Sometimes the "promotion" was masked as a "re-organization", a shuffling around of responsibilities. In reality, this sleight of hand was nothing but an avoidance of decision-making and effective leading – a making real of the Peter Principle. Instead of frankly counseling a no longer satisfactory manager to improve or move on, the CEO copped-out. Was it all about "saving face"? Depends on whose face is being saved.

Regardless, the employees (the frogs) who get the "demoted" boss have to deal with his stomping around and other behaviors stemming from the so-called "severity error"; when someone is treated shabbily by superiors, he treats his subordinates poorly, a form of "down stream retribution".

And, worse for the organization, the demoted boss's new group knows full well it, too, has been down-graded.

My Thoughts

114

Lubans

Rocks & Change*

 o not trust rocks. A rock resting on the rim of the Grand Canyon may give an impression of strength and permanence but as soon as a man turns his back the rock will resume disintegrating and sneaking off to California. And it is not only that particular rock that is unreliable. Every rock everywhere is growing smaller or larger, rising up or sinking down, or creeping about the planet in a scandalous manner.

I use this quote to set a context for my classroom discussion of the changes underway in higher education – something that has been happening for three or more decades, prompted by the Internet.

What does a quote about geology have to do with the modern organization? Quite a bit. When change is upon us, it is good to realize change is unavoidable, inevitable – even in the landscape. Any time we find ourselves certain that the old way of doing something is OK, think again.

---

* Editor at Time Life Books. Quoted in Readings from the Hurricane Island Outward Bound School, Edited by Alison Murray Kuller, June 1986. Rockland Maine, HIOBS. p. 59.

Lubans

The Rope and the Cleat

*ittin' On The Dock Of The Bay*, the cleat was berating a rope tied to a boat: "You are such a wuss, you give in and surrender to the waves; you are a real slacker! And you, unlike me, are easily cut in two. An iron bar between me and the boat would be much stronger and safer; anything would be better than a slinky like you to face the storm's winds and waves!"

A fisherman, overhearing the cleat's tirade, began to think (not his strong suit) that the cleat was right. With the coming storm a rigid iron bar would be better than a flimsy rope. While he should have known better, he went ahead and cast aside the ropes and replaced them with iron bars, secured with D-rings to the boat at one end and to the cleat at the other.

A storm came up that night and was gone by the morning – along with the boat! When the sad fisherman looked down into the murky water dockside he saw his sunken boat with its starboard side impaled by the two iron bars. The cleat, torn out when the boat sank, was still attached with its D-ring to the iron bar.

And so it is at work when the adamant opponent of change finds herself slowly sinking below the waves, going down with the boat instead of working towards change. We should aspire to be like the rope and dip with the waves, emulate the movement of the wave, judiciously accommodating and riding out the storm. Be able – like we are advised in the Thirty-six Stratagems -to win without battle, "use the enemy's own strength against him."

My Thoughts

" Use the enemy's own strength against him.

Aesop

The Wolf and the Housedog

 Wolf, meeting a big well-fed Mastiff with a wooden collar about his neck asked him who it was that fed him so well and yet compelled him to drag that heavy log about wherever he went. "The master," he replied. Then said the Wolf: "May no friend of mine ever be in such a plight; for the weight of this chain is enough to spoil the appetite."

Caxton's epimythium for this fable: "Therfore there is no rychesse gretter than lyberte / For lyberte is better than alle the gold of the world."

Reminds me of when I stayed in a job that was no longer a match for my democratic style and skills. While I had had a very good first five years (in NASCAR terms, a "great ride") in developing teams that did outstanding work, the next five were fairly dismal, each passing year like a tight collar around my neck, chafing. I should have been out the door during the 6th year, but figured, delusionally, it would all work out. It didn't and became progressively worse as new administrators came on board. The newbies were top down traditionalistas; I began to feel like I was "behind enemy lines". Why did I put up with a bad boss, unsupportive colleagues, and a now-boring job?

All the obvious reasons mostly summed up in the word, security. The wolf would have none of it. Save the wolves!

My Thoughts

Lubans

The Fallen Tree

he night storm had wreaked havoc. Deep in the forest, the pelting rain and driving wind had toppled one of the mightiest trees, a monarch of the forest. It'd been sent crashing down onto the forest floor, mortally wounded.

The trees and forest animals gathered to mourn; they surrounded the tree. They looked anxiously about, worried if other storms would come and destroy their land. They worried about their own future. How would they get along without their old friend, its high branches, its corrugated bark, its shade on hot days and its shelter during the cold and wet times?

The fallen tree, with a sigh like that of a gentle wind through leaves, asked: "What do you see?"

The gathered trees and animals look around. "We see the destruction from the storm, the land is torn. We see your bruised body and shattered limbs."

The fallen tree whispered again, "What do you see?"

The mourners wondered to themselves, "What's more to see?"

Then, "Wait, wait", cried one of the smallest trees. "Look up! I can see the sun, I can see the sky. The forest is now open to the sky."

"Yes, yes", sighed the fallen tree. "I soon will be gone, but the sun, our mother, will shine down to the forest floor and the young will thrive."

And so it is, when organizations wax anxious about the departure of a workplace luminary, someone upon whom the sun had shined more than most. We are often encouraged, seemingly obligated, to make dissuading counter-offers.

I always shook that person's hand and wished him good luck in his decision to leave. Sure, that person was irreplaceable, but I wasn't going to replace that person. I was going to find someone new, someone who would bring fresh ideas and new perspectives, someone who would come out of the canopy's shade and grow and aspire to be as grand in her own way as that irreplaceable star.

My Thoughts

Aesop

The Frogs and the Well

wo Frogs lived together in a marsh. But one hot summer the marsh dried up, and they left it to look for another place to live in: for frogs like damp places if they can get them. By and by they came to a deep well, and one of them looked down into it, and said to the other, 'This looks a nice cool place, let us jump in and settle here.' But the other, who had a wiser head on his shoulders, replied, 'Not so fast, my friend, supposing this well dried up like the marsh, how should we get out again? '

Think twice before you act.

Wise advice, certainly. But then what about, "He who hesitates is lost?" Or, "Nothing ventured, nothing gained?"

Permit me to add a revisionist ending: Out of the blue, an observant owl swooped down on the debating frogs, seized one in his claws and soared off. Panicked, the other frog leaped high, right into the open mouth of an attentive fox!

And so it goes sometimes in the workplace, as we dither and put off decisions. Sometimes, we seem wedded to the notion of never "riding a wild horse into the sun"!*

* "Ride A Wild Horse" by Hannah Kahn (1911–1988).

In my profession – perhaps others – it is considered good practice for a task force to list out all relevant questions about the feasibility of implementing a new way of work or service. We, assiduously, list out and debate the pros and the cons, the plusses and minuses of making the decision. The un-prioritized minuses usually exceed the plusses by a ratio of 10:1. The more minuses (reasons not to change) the more satisfied the task force members. Answering the what-if's (some would stump Athena!) and anticipating the worst-case scenarios drain the task force's time and energy. Inevitably, the deadline – if there is one – passes. The task force then takes decisive action: "We need more time for further study!"

I discovered a remedy to indecision. I, the Great Unknowing Being, told them I'd make the decision if they did not in 24 hours. Can you guess the outcome?

A better adage: "Everything in moderation, including moderation," except when you are on that wild horse!

My Thoughts

" Everything in moderation, including moderation.

Chapter 5

Budgeting and strategic planning

The Grasshopper Saves for a Rainy Day!

e all know the story, the Ant and the Grass-hopper – it is probably one of Aesop's best-known fables. The grasshopper fiddles away his summer and starves in the winter. The industrious ant – not to be diverted from storing food by the grasshopper's sweet music – has the last (literally) laugh. It's a harsh lesson for the grasshopper.

Well, that fable suggests the adage: Saving for a rainy day. The notion derives from farming. There will be times when the blue bird of happiness absconds and you find yourself shoeless on a dirt road with nothing for market. That's why farmers save for a rainy day.

Herb Kelleher, Southwest Airlines' former CEO, had this to say in a presentation at the Stanford Business School about "managing in good times for the bad": "We figure there's going to be at least two crises in every decade, and we'd better be ready for them. My slogan has always been, 'We manage in good times so that we'll do well in bad times.'"

Indicative of Southwest's resilience and anticipation was its being the first airline back in American skies after the terrorist assaults in

September of 2001. Mr. Kelleher offers us good advice. Unfortunately, too few of us see the storm clouds gathering while we enjoy the clear skies of a seemingly perfect climate. Changing for the better is doubly hard in good times. "If it ain't broke, don't fix it", is the all too-ready refrain to keep the status quo. So, one of the most challenging parts in leadership is keeping an organization focused on getting better, wisely using all of its resources and avoiding waste even when it does not have to. Once ingrained, that mindset will serve us well when the bad times come.

My Thoughts

Lubans

The Dog and the Stick

nce upon a time there was a dog who loved to chase and fetch sticks in the forest. But, the dog did not like surrendering the stick so it could be thrown again. It would run off with the stick, jutting out of its mouth, settle down some distance from the master, its tail motoring, and chew and chew on the stick until it was in bits, This happened each day, for weeks, and months. Eventually there were no more sticks – it was a small forest – and the master shrugged helplessly when the dog bounced up and down to persuade him to throw a stick, any stick – there were no more to be found. The forest was bare. They went home, unhappily.

And so it is with any resource. Mind that you do not use it all up; no matter how much fun you have in doing so, in chewing on that bone. Always leave some for the next day, for the next week, the next month and the next generation of dogs and masters.

Aesop

The Flying Beetle*

Chapter 5
Budgeting and strategic planning
Exceeding your resources

here was once a beetle who lived in a dung heap. One day when he had eaten his fill, he crawled out from under the dung, looked up, and saw an eagle soaring high in the air, flying swiftly by. This made the beetle feel disgusted with himself and his way of life, so he said to the other beetles, "Do you see that eagle! He flies so quickly and he is so strong, with a sharp beak and deadly talons. He can rise up to the clouds or come racing back down to earth as he pleases. We beetles are so pathetic by comparison: we fly, but we're not birds, and we're not like the other bugs either. Yet when I raise my voice, it resounds like the eagle's cry, and I shine as brightly as the eagle does.

No more dung heap for me! I am going to join the company of birds and fly together with them wherever they go, an equal in their ranks!" The beetle then flew upwards, letting forth a mighty cry that was actually just a nasty buzzing sound. He pursued the eagle high above the clouds, but the strong winds were too much for him, and he came crashing back to the ground, weak and shaken, far from the dung heap that was his home. Unable to find anything to eat, the little beetle lamented, "They can call me a bird or a bug, I don't care, just so long as I find my way back home to my dung heap!"

* For a more literal translation, see Source, Laura Gibbs' Oxford Aesop 332.

Arrogance leads to disaster. If you pretend to be someone you are not, no one will respect you, and you will end up worse off than you were to begin with.

The concluding moral evokes, for me, the vainly envious worker who wants a higher job in spite of a lack of experience or qualifications. There's no question he'd be in over his head, but that does not get in the way of his ambition: "The eagle (the leader) has all the perks, why not me?"

I recall in my study of a woman's basketball team that one of the players – who was not happy with "riding the pine" as a sub – left the program to go to another team. There she was promised a starring role; no more waiting on the bench! Alas, her inconsistent play – flashes of brilliance followed by stretches of mishandling the ball – got worse due to the extra stress of being a starter/leader.

Yet, there's something to be said about climbing out of a seeming "dung-heap" to higher levels, to taking a chance, to betting on your own success.

Or, we may choose a prestigious job that pays well but offers few challenges. It's routine and comfortable, but, to our dismay, the organization likes the status quo: routine and comfortable! And, it resents being reminded about its shortcomings. Let's hope, like the beetle, when we fall back to earth, to reality, we're wiser for when the next opportunity comes knocking.

Aesop

The Cowardly Lion

Bull-Frog, according to rule,
Sat a-croak in his usual pool:
And he laughed in his heart
As a Lion did start,
In a fright from the brink like a fool.

Imaginary fears are the worst.

In another telling of this fable*, the facetious frog does not guffaw with impunity:

The lion had come to the river to take a drink when he heard a strange, rumbling sound. He looked around, but he could see no one. He stood there, listening, and then he heard the rumbling sound again, and he trembled with fear. At last he saw a bullfrog emerging from the river's waters. He realized it had been the frog making that sound all along, and so he crushed the frog beneath his paws.

This fable is for someone who talks big but does nothing. So, mind your unexamined words, lest they get you "crushed". Sometimes being a jackass will get you kicked.

* For a more literal translation see in Sources, Laura Gibbs' Oxford Aesop 270.

Aesop

The Frogs Asking for a King

Chapter 5
Budgeting and strategic planning
When more is less

he Frogs, grieved at having no established Ruler, sent ambassadors to Jupiter entreating for a King. Perceiving their simplicity, he cast down a huge log into the lake. The Frogs were terrified at the splash occasioned by its fall and hid themselves in the depths of the pool. But as soon as they realized that the huge log was motionless, they swam again to the top of the water, dismissed their fears, climbed up, and began squatting on it in contempt. After some time they began to think themselves ill-treated in the appointment of so inert a Ruler, and sent a second deputation to Jupiter to pray that he would set over them another sovereign. He then gave them an Eel to govern them. When the Frogs discovered his easy good nature, they sent yet a third time to Jupiter to beg him to choose for them still another King. Jupiter, displeased with all their complaints, sent a Heron, who preyed upon the Frogs day by day till there were none left to croak upon the lake.

A good story for those who have no time for a Democratic Workplace, who love the hierarchy, the bureaucracy. Imagine the joys we experience in being ruled by a desk (bureau!).

Only a strong boss will do for some. Why? Why not self rule for the formerly free frogs? The leader that promises all manner of good things if elected, well, he or she could be a heron in disguise, or more Aesopically, a wolf in sheep's clothing.

My Thoughts

" Imagine the joys we experience in being ruled by a desk.

Aesop

The Trees and the Axe

Woodman went into the forest and begged of the Trees the favour of a handle for his Axe. The principal Trees at once agreed to so modest a request, and unhesitatingly gave him a young ash sapling, out of which he fashioned the handle he desired. No sooner had he done so than he set to work to fell the noblest Trees in the wood. When they saw the use to which he was putting their gift, they cried, "Alas! alas! We are undone, but we are ourselves to blame. The little we gave has cost us all: had we not sacrificed the rights of the ash, we might ourselves have stood for ages."

In my 9-5 working days, some of what I did – like streamlining and reducing complexity – was viewed akin to the trees giving an ax handle to the woodcutter. One of my daily battle cries was to reduce backlogs. "He Never Met a Backlog He Liked" would serve well as my career's epitaph. Many of my peers would do well under another: "They Never Met A Backlog They Didn't Like." You see, I took to heart the adage: Save the time of the user."

If librarians had anything like "pissing contests" one of them was for bragging rights to the largest backlog, some numbering in the millions of unprocessed materials. They believed, among a multitude of lofty reasons, that a backlog was a good thing, a positive like inventoried factory orders; a guarantee there'd be work (and a raison d'être) into the next millennium. My take was that backlogs were a burden to the library and soured our relationships with readers and administrators. Backlogged, unavailable books, and other bottlenecks, congested access lanes, tied up beaucoup bucks in maintenance, created delays for readers, and harmed the image of the library and librarian as information provider.

I was not arming the woodcutter. In my day, every improvement, every backlog eliminated, resulted in freed up budget dollars for other library purposes; you see, we got to keep the money we saved. Not long after I'd left library land, higher powers applied mandatory budget cuts and forced previously unwilling managers to reduce expenses. The forced streamlining – a form of hostage taking: reduce costs, keep you job – did result in improvements, but the savings were surrendered to the central university budget to pay for more "with-it" programs, like an Olympic-size hot tub for the student union. While many of my former peers kept their jobs, the woodcutter was now loose in the library.

Abstemius

The Mice and the Oak

he Mice found it so troublesom to be still climbing the Oak for every Bit they put in their Bellies, that they were once to set their Teeth to't, and bring the Acorns down to them; but some wiser than some, and a Grave Experienc'd Mouse, bad them have a care what they did; for it we destroy our Nurse at present, who shall feed us hereafter!

Resolution without Foresight is but a Temerarious Folly: And the Consequences of Things are the first Point to be taken into Consideration.

The "Grave Experienc'd Mouse" has got it right. We deforest the land at our own risk just like we do when, presumptuously, we rush through a policy without considering worst-case scenarios. And, acts of "Temerarious Folly" arm the naysayers, those who resist change regardless of necessity. They point to the unintended consequences of the past as sufficient reason to do nothing.

Aesop

The Lark and the Farmer

Lark nested in a field of corn, and was rearing her brood under cover of the ripening grain. One day, before the young were fully fledged, the Farmer came to look at the crop, and, finding it yellowing fast, he said, "I must send round word to my neighbours to come and help me reap this field." One of the young Larks overheard him, and was very much frightened, and asked her mother whether they hadn't better move house at once. "There's no hurry," replied she; "a man who looks to his friends for help will take his time about a thing." In a few days the Farmer came by again, and saw that the grain was overripe and falling out of the ears upon the ground. "I must put it off no longer," he said; "This very day I'll hire the men and set them to work at once." The Lark heard him and said to her young, "Come, my children, we must be off: he talks no more of his friends now, but is going to take things in hand himself."

Self-help is the best help.

At work, I could always count on a few people who helped promptly and some others who sort of helped. Most staff, regardless if there was a crisis demanding "all hands on deck", were always too busy to pitch in. It was not until we paid for the extra hours that we saw interest in helping. Perhaps I should have demonstrated more urgency as to why the work needed to be done. When the mother lark spoke, the chicks knew it was time to go – the urgency was real. Some leaders cry wolf, exaggerate , or even lie. You might get away with it once like Aesop's boy, but, if you depend on cooperation and collaboration to confront a crisis, you'll be the loser.

My Thoughts

Aesop

The Woman and Her Hen

Woman possessed a Hen that gave her an egg every day. She often pondered how she might obtain two eggs daily instead of one, and at last, to gain her purpose, determined to give the Hen a double allowance of barley. From that day the Hen became fat and sleek, and never once laid another egg.

Aesop's Woman was not a disciple of less being more. Her hen's liking of luxury may give credence to the notion of "too much of a good thing".

But, being a contrarian, here's another view:

Daryle Singletary writes,

"Too much fun, what's that mean?

It's like too much money, there's no such thing

It's like a girl too pretty with too much class

Being too lucky, a car too fast

No matter what they say, I've done

But I ain't never had too much fun."

Yet, on the job, I know managers are expected to appear fastidiously frugal and resolutely resourceful. I recall how my going on a paid trip to a conference in Honolulu garnered tsk, tsk'ing and plenty of askance looks.

Budget managers are all about making sure we never have too much fun. That may be a "bean counter's" chief chore. The bean counter (BC) thinks it is her responsibility to make sure there's barely enough, and most definitely, not too much. For the BC, less is indeed more, all the while pinching our pennies.

When I teach budgeting I refer to Aaron Wildavsky's work on budgetary behavior and BC thinking. Some of the latter is illogical and inimical to the best use of budgetary resources:

• "Substantial carryover (a surplus) indicates that the agency does not need as much as it received and cuts will be made in the future." So, if you have streamlined, reduced expenses and saved your organization's money, that excess money is hoovered up into the general fund and does not return to your unit (unless you have gotten special permission from the BC or, much better, his superior).

• "Suspicion is raised if the agency comes out even, the budget ends on zero. It is, strangely enough, seen as spending to the limit without considering the need for economy." So, library friends and colleagues, when you rush to zero out the fiscal year by buying ultra expensive sets of materials that will likely never be used, keep in mind that the BC already knows about this scam, everyone does it. No wonder there's never any money for the really important stuff!

• "If the agency runs out of funds it may be accused of coercive deficiency trying to compel more funds on the grounds that a vital activity will suffer." A very risky process, unless you are protected from the top. In any case, those who have to pay for your debauchery will detest you, but then you may not care!

Chapter 6
The effective follower

La Fontaine

The Head and the Tail
of the Serpent

 he Snake has two parts, it is said,
Hostile to man—his tail and head;
And both, as all of us must know,
Are well known to the Fates below.
Once on a time a feud arose
For the precedence—almost blows.
"I always walked before the Tail,"
So said the Head, without avail.
The Tail replied, "I travel o'er
Furlongs and leagues—ay, score on score—
Just as I please. Then, is it right
I should be always in this plight!
Jove! I am sister, and not slave:
Equality is all I crave.
Both of the selfsame blood, I claim
Our treatment, then, should be the same.
As well as her I poison bear,
Powerful and prompt, for men to fear.
And this is all I wish to ask;
Command it—'tis a simple task:

Let me but in my turn go first;
For her 'twill be no whit the worst.
I sure can guide, as well as she;
No subject for complaint shall be."
Heaven was cruel in consenting:
Such favours lead but to repenting.
Jove should be deaf to such wild prayers:
He was not then; so first she fares;
She, who in brightest day saw not,
No more than shut up in a pot,
Struck against rocks, and many a tree—
'Gainst passers-by, continually;
Until she led them both, you see,
Straight into Styx. Unhappy all
Those wretched states who, like her, fall."

Keeping to my contrarian ways, I'd add that both leader (head) and follower (tail) need to have a sense of direction. It's what Mary Parker Follett said many years ago when describing effective leadership:

"Leader and followers are both following the invisible leader – the common purpose." When students do the "balloon trolley" – which I use to teach the importance of shared leadership – I choose leaders from the back and the front and the middle to help a group navigate around the classroom or hallway or parking lot. Keeping things interesting are the balloons in front and back of each member of the trolley. Drop one and start over. As each newly appointed leader keeps his/her place in the line and directs the group, the lessons are quickly learned. Each member of the group, regardless of location, has a role and responsibility, the least of which is to listen and to speak up (communicate!) when the line encounters difficulty – the tail indeed has information which the head does not. The linking metaphor is not lost on the group – each literally must support the other.

La Fontaine's version of this fable, in-line with Aesop, suggests that letting the "tail", the rabble, lead a nation will result in disaster. A century after La Fontaine, many would dispute the divine right of kings and some would embrace the revolutionary notion of governance "of the people, by the people, for the people." Yet, even today, many bosses, the world over, are reluctant to embrace a democratic leadership. It's a bit like the centuries it took for scholars to get over the "ancient mistake in natural history" that a snake's tail was as poisonous as the head!

My Thoughts

La Fontaine

The Jay in the Feathers of the Peacock

 peacock moulted: soon a jay was seen
Bedeck'd with Argus tail of gold and green,
High strutting, with elated crest,
As much a peacock as the rest.
His trick was recognized and bruited,
His person jeer'd at, hiss'd, and hooted.
The peacock gentry flock'd together,
And pluck'd the fool of every feather.
Nay more, when back he sneak'd to join his race,
They shut their portals in his face."
"There is another sort of jay,
The number of its legs the same,
Which makes of borrow'd plumes display,
And plagiary is its name.
But hush! the tribe I'll not offend;
'Tis not my work their ways to mend.

Notably, at fable's end, LaFontaine targets plagiarists. To which "tribe" is he is referring? Academics? Or is he targeting the Parisian equivalent of London's Fleet Street? Or, is his complaint in general of anyone, like Aesop's jay, who feathers his cap with feathers (achievements) lifted from others?

For scholars, the most blatant "plagiary" is straightforward copying without attribution. In the workplace, this is akin to taking full personal credit for someone else's good ideas or work. And, then there's the sly supervisor who attributes the good work to her department but omits naming the individual(s) most responsible.

Equally petty and unsavory is when someone imitates another's ideas, recasts them somewhat, but gives no tip of the hat to the originator. Interestingly, a professed oblivion is often the case with hardcore plagiarists, people who've ripped off pages of someone else's work almost word for word. When confronted, they deny, shift blame, obfuscate, and often threaten to sue. Since many academic plagiarists won't apologize for stealing – nor will their peers "out" them – I understand why LaFontaine ends his commentary with "'Tis not my work their ways to mend."

My Thoughts

Odo of Cheriton

The Two Monks*

here were two monks who were on a journey, and along the way they came to a monastery. One of the monks, an inveterate liar, exclaimed, 'Let's make a bet! By telling lies, I will be able to make more profit here than you and your truth-telling.' The other monk, who always told the truth, agreed to the wager. They then went into the monastery, only to find that it was full of apes. The liar saluted the community of apes, and the abbot of the apes inquired, 'What do you think of me and my brethren?' The liar replied, 'I have never seen a religious community so fair as this one. As I gaze upon you, I realize that men are not superior to apes, but the other way around: you apes are the ideal to which we should aspire.' And so he continued to praise the apes, and the apes, greatly pleased, gave him gold and silver and other precious gifts. Then the abbot of the apes asked the other man, 'What do you think of me and my brethren?' The monk replied truthfully, saying, 'I have never seen a congregation that looked so ridiculous or smelled so bad.' The apes grew angry and attacked the man, beating him so badly that he barely escaped with his life.

Telling the truth can be a risky business.

---

* For a more literal translation see Sources, Jacobs Odo 41, "Two Brothers: Against Flatterers."; also Laura Gibbs' Oxford Aesop 108.

We know from research on effective followers – self-starters who do not have to be led – a willingness to tell the truth can be dangerous to one's health, particularly with an apish audience. About half the time, effective followers are punished for doing a really good job.

While screen-writing in the Hollywood of the 1930s, P. G. Wodehouse, saw a lot of another type of follower/flatterer: The Yes Man. His short story "The Nodder" explains:

"A Nodder is something like a Yes-man, only lower in the social scale. A Yes-Man's duty is to attend conferences and say 'Yes.' A Nodder's, as the name implies, is to nod. The chief executive throws some statement of opinion and looks about him expectantly. This is the cue for the senior Yes-Man to say yes. He is followed, in order of precedence, by the second Yes-Man – or Vice-Yesser -, as he sometimes is called- and the junior Yes-Man. Only when all the Yes-Men have yessed, do the Nodders begin to function. They nod."

Aesop

Hercules and the Wagoner

 carter was driving a wagon along a country lane, when the wheels sank down deep into a rut. The rustic driver, stupefied and aghast, stood looking at the wagon, and did nothing but utter loud cries to Hercules to come and help him. Hercules, it is said, appeared and thus addressed him: "Put your shoulders to the wheels, my man. Goad on your bullocks, and never more pray to me for help, until you have done your best to help yourself, or depend upon it you will henceforth pray in vain."

Self-help is the best help.

Akin to the proverbial "The Lord helps those who help themselves", I, too, have seen wishful thinking (consider strategic planning) sometimes replace purposeful doing. Often, it seems – given the miniscule results – we do planning exercises since it beats working. Or, we may find ourselves paralyzed by a gargantuan project. I recall having to lead an effort not unlike our Hero's cleaning out the Augean Stables. Where I worked had huge and historic backlogs; many believed these logjams were too large to deal with without more staff and time, as much as five years. I told the staff there would be no new staff and that we needed to start today to do something, indeed, anything! So, we broke the project down into monthly goals – reasonable and measurable – and then started doing. Not surprisingly, we exceeded the monthly goals and after a year and a half we'd mastered the backlog beast. A cause for celebrating – and we did – leavened a bit with the resentment exhibited by some of the people most responsible for the backlogs. (See Aesop's "Fox and the Sour Grapes")

My Thoughts

Group 5*

The Fox Gets Left Behind

nce upon a time the animals tried to build a balloon to travel to the Animal Conference. Almost all of the animals took part in the building. For three days and nights they worked. The Spider created net, the Elephant blew air (into the balloon), etc., but one animal, the Fox, went to a spa resort to see the "fur dresser" so as to look good before the long flight. In the end, all the animals climbed into the basket, but the balloon could not fly (get up) – it was too heavy. The group leader called all the animals together and said: 'While almost everyone worked well, but we are just a little bit too heavy. Can you guess who is not going with us!'

"We have rowed well,' said the Flea as the fishing boat arrived at its mooring." – Latvian Proverb

---

Like L'Estrange's self-important fly – "What a Dust do I raise! says the Fly upon the Coach-Wheel? and what a rate do I drive at, says the same Fly again upon the Horse's Buttock?" – the fox assigns herself an underserved elevated position, making her personal appearance more important than helping build the balloon.

* Group 5: Evita Stankeviča; Lana Augule; Inga Vovčenko; Tamāra Černišova; Ilona Vēliņa-Švilpe; Ieva Krūmiņa; Viktorija Moskina.

We may think we are important – which, of course, we are – but we are not that important when group effort is needed. The supercilious fox is like Aesop's grasshopper who idles away the summer and starves in winter.

But, let's not forget the fox's perspective; her looking good, adding a touch of class to the group, has its merits.

My Thoughts

Krylov

The Swan, the Pike, and the Crab

hene'er companions don't agree,
They work without accord;
And naught but trouble doth result,
Although they all work hard.

One day a swan, a pike, a crab,
Resolved a load to haul;
All three were harnessed to the cart,
And pulled together all.

But though they pulled with all their might,
The cart-load on the bank stuck tight.
The swan pulled upward to the skies;
The crab did backward crawl;
The pike made for the water straight —
It proved no use at all!

Now, which of them was most to blame
'Tis not for me to say;
But this I know: the load is there
Unto this very day.

No doubt, there's an easy solution: a kick-ass leader to bring this transfixed trio in line! Yes, a muleteer's whip would get the job done, but why do not the swan, pike and crab cooperate? Do they (and us) always need to be told what to do?

Had they cooperated, the metaphoric cart would have moved on. Probably Krylov's point is that some people are never going to cooperate, "without accord"; hence "the load is there unto this very day."

While we all offer different talents in a group effort, it makes good sense to establish Role and Purpose, two quintessential rules for group development. When work groups were at odds, I saw our organization's cart bog down. Neither collaboration, compromise nor consensus was possible, leaving outcomes purely to chance. Who to cut the Gordian knot?

I just heard about a German city with 5 boroughs, each with its own public library system. None cooperate; they all stand alone. Germany has a literacy rate approaching 99.9% so these five libraries would see increased use (a desirable) were they to cooperate, pool resources, and create a single library card for readers.

Predictably, these library systems will be forced to consolidate and the readers and the libraries will be the worse for it. It's like the s-shaped curve. When you are on the rise (daffodils a-bloom and skies are blue), that's when you should be looking for the next upward curve, the next big improvement. When you are on the declining slope, it's too late; you'll have settle for whatever someone on the outside hands you and that's only if they want to.

La Fontaine

The Sun and the Frogs

ejoicing on their tyrant's wedding-day,
The people drown'd their care in drink;
While from the general joy did Aesop shrink,
And show'd its folly in this way.
"The sun," said he, "once took it in his head
To have a partner for his bed."
From swamps, and ponds, and marshy bogs,
Up rose the wailings of the frogs.
"What shall we do, should he have progeny?"
Said they to Destiny;
"One sun we scarcely can endure,
And half-a-dozen, we are sure,
Will dry the very sea.
Adieu to marsh and fen!
Our race will perish then,
Or be obliged to fix
Their dwelling in the Styx!"
For such an humble animal,
The frog, I take it, reason'd well.

La Fontaine's poetic retelling of Aesop's fable has an unusual structure. He begins with a drunken celebration of a tyrant's (Louis XIV) wedding and slips in a dismayed Aesop who explains why the hoi-polloi should be wary not merry. The poem concludes with the climate-change-minded frogs realizing that if one "sun" is enough to dry up their pond, then a few more radiant stars will lead to certain doom.

My original take on this fable was related to a tendency in some organizations to "procreate" like-mindedness among its employees resulting in low innovation and tentative decision-making. The cliché, "the acorn does not fall far from the tree", pretty much encapsulates this phenomenon.

I am also reminded of recent research in which the more like-minded a group, the greater the probability it will polarize into groupthink. It gets worse. When a group is like-minded in extreme ways – no, it is not a condition unique to violent extremists but applies as well to hidebound members of very traditional organizations – that like-mindedness will polarize into a suicidal resistance to change and a willingness (among violent extremists) to perpetrate even worse atrocities.

In the workplace (innovative or traditional) we can counter groupthink through leadership that celebrates alternative thinking, that supports people with opposing points of view and that welcomes and defends differences. And, an organization that eschews groupthink deliberately recruits people who think critically, are independent in decision-making, and possess a bias for action.

Aesop

The Ass, the Cock, and the Lion

n Ass and a Cock were in a straw-yard to-gether when a Lion, desperate from hunger, approached the spot. He was about to spring upon the Ass, when the Cock (to the sound of whose voice the Lion, it is said, has a singular aversion) crowed loudly, and the Lion fled away as fast as he could. The Ass, observing his trepidation at the mere crowing of a Cock summoned courage to attack him, and galloped after him for that purpose. He had run no long distance, when the Lion, turning about, seized him and tore him to pieces.

False confidence often leads into danger.

Or as Sir Roger L'Estrange has it: "The Force of Unaccountable Aversions, is Insuperable. The Fool that is Wise and Brave only in his Own Conceit, runs on without Fear or Wit; but Noise does no Bus'ness."

And so it is at work. Aesop touches on one of the biggest mistakes an individual or team can make: An overweening optimism.

We humans are just as prone to "false confidence" as is the rooster. This is but one of the biases blighting group work. Like-minded people are especially vulnerable to "group-think" – the failure to hear or respect contrarian views against a dominant opinion, regardless what the data may be showing.

I saw this up close and personal multiple times when I presented findings about student use of the Internet to library groups in the late 90s and early 2000s. As the users' independent use of e-resources rapidly grew, library services developed for a print-only world dwindled. My research may have been heard but it was not listened to – a few huffed there was no need to innovate or to adapt services – but my predictions pretty much came to be. Eventually, due to pressure from outside, including from with-it library users, waves of emulation – started by a few genuine innovations – soon began to ripple across library-land.

Groupthink can and often does – when the stakes are truly high – propel us toward disaster. Since Aesop's animals can talk, why does the rooster not warn the ass about his false assumption?

"Come back, you dumb ass! It's my crowing, not your braying!"

Every group needs at least a few members ready to speak up when over-confidence rears its supercilious head.

My Thoughts

Lubans

How the Rat Got Its Tail

he animals, including man, who store food petitioned Zeus for help. It was about rat's stealing the grain and nuts they'd gathered against the harsh times of winter.

The animals said it was not fair that the rat could sneak into locked storerooms and munch away on the food they'd accumulated through their planning and diligence. And, the rat was hard to spot; practiced in stealth, he could slip past and through most barriers. Once in, he'd chew in silence and then tiptoe away, leaving only his droppings and a depleted storeroom.

Zeus asked rat, "Have you been stealing?" Rat lied and denied. At the time of this story, the rat had no tail. Zeus doubted rat and, in his wisdom, gave the rat a tail, a long hairless one. The rat saw this as a reward and was proud of his new look, but quickly grew to regret it. Now when you go by a storage closet and see a little bit of a tail sticking out from under the door, you know who's there. You can yank that giveaway tail and make the rat squeal and scrabble.

Moral: Taking too much for granted can get you in big trouble and sooner than you might think.

Aesop

The Tortoise and the Eagle

A Tortoise, discontented with his lowly life, and envious of the birds he saw disporting themselves in the air, begged an Eagle to teach him to fly. The Eagle protested that it was idle for him to try, as nature had not provided him with wings; but the Tortoise pressed him with entreaties and promises of treasure, insisting that it could only be a question of learning the craft of the air. So at length the Eagle consented to do the best he could for him, and picked him up in his talons. Soaring with him to a great height in the sky he then let him go, and the wretched Tortoise fell headlong and was dashed to pieces on a rock.

Sometimes, when you think you are ready to "disport" yourself in a top-level job, it's best you don't. You may not be ready to fly at that level and it is a kindness, not a cruelty, when someone stops you.

Early in my career, I'd wax impatient with rules about tenure or years of experience. It all felt like thwart and stifle, an excuse to deny my ambition simply because of my age. Looking back, I am glad I did not always get my way and in some instances I regret that I did.

So, you may be willing and able but you may not be ready.

One version of this fable gives the eagle an ulterior motive. He drops the turtle from on high onto a pile of rocks and then dines leisurely and sumptuously on the remains. Someone who facilitates your premature ambition may not be doing so in your best interests.

My Thoughts

Group 2*

Cat and Mouse

nce upon a time there lived a Cat and a Mouse. As they knew each other from early childhood they were very close friends. But one day the Cat's instincts took over – the Cat suddenly grabbed the Mouse and ate it. The next morning the Cat went out to meet his friend – but there was nobody to greet him....

Once you've cut the bread, you cannot put it together again. – Latvian Proverb.

A poignantly sad story of friendship lost, one friend surrenders to base instinct and gobbles up his little buddy.

How often do we say or do things we regret? I recall early in my career, as a manager of several branches, calling up a satellite branch and ordering the assistant to correct a customer's perceived wrong. I may even have bullied the hapless assistant, "Do you know who I am?" and ordered the change. Shortly after, I heard from the head of the branch in brisk terms what he thought of my high-handedness. He was right.

Sure, I apologized, but like cut bread, the loaf cannot be made whole.

* Group 2: Gunta Dogžina; Ludmila Macpane; Aina Štrāle; Viktorija Surska; Vēsma Klūga; Irēna Morīte.

165

Lubans

The Ahead-of-His-Time Carpenter Bee

ong ago, when animals could talk, a drowsy carpenter bee emerged from his tunnel-nest. While winter, this afternoon was unusually warm.

He breathed in the warm air, buzzed around a bit, did a somersault in the sunshine, and happily droned off looking for nectar.

Then winter clouds slid across the sky, chilling the air. Our bee's movements slowed and slowed; his zooming efforts to get home went nowhere. It was too late. As he collapsed onto the deck below the nest, he was heard to mutter:

"Being first is not all it's made out to be!"

That night a gentle snow blanketed the bee.

And, so it can be at work. While there may be glory in being first, you may find yourself all alone. What was urgent for you may not be so for anyone else.

In the late 90s, I did one of the first studies on student Internet use – at least for library-land. I thought the results were pretty dramatic so I decided against publishing my conclusions in the conventional print way; instead I made the draft report and data available on my web page – it is still there. For a while my approach worked, earning a mention in the NY Times and some speaking engagements. And, since it was on the Internet at the peak of the dotcom boom, lots of non-library types expressed interest – what I had to say mattered more to them than to my librarian colleagues who did not share my urgency about the findings.

Not long after, others joined in the research and my humble early efforts were pretty much forgotten. I have to wonder if I had published in a "legacy" print journal, indexed and abstracted, whether the research would not have had more of a wider and lasting impact.

My Thoughts

" While there may be glory in being first, you may find yourself all alone.

Abstemius

The Ass's Wish

n Ass was wishing in a hard Winter, for a little warm Weather, and a Mouthful of fresh Grass to knap upon, in Exchange for a heartless Truss of Straw, and a cold Lodging. In good time, the warm Weather, and the fresh Grass comes on; but so much Toil and Bus'ness along with it, that the Ass grows quickly as sick of the Spring, as he was of the Winter. His next Longing is for Summer; but what with Harvest-Work, and other Drudgeries of that Season, he is worse now than he was in the Spring and then he fancies he shall never be well 'till Autumn comes: But there again, what with carrying Apples, Grapes, Fewel, Winter-Provisions, etc. he finds himself in a greater Hurry than ever. In fine, when he has trod the Circle of the Year in a Course of restless Labour, his last Prayer is for Winter again; and that he may but take up his Rest where he began his Complaint.

The Life of an unsteady Man runs away in a Course of vain Wishes, and unprofitable Repentance: An unsettled Mind can never be at rest. There's no Season without its Bus'ness.

Is Abstemius' moral unduly harsh in its blaming the "unsteady Man" for his "vain Wishes", his "unprofitable Repentance" because, after all, "There's no Season without its Bus'ness."

This fable (from the 15th century) suggests a variety of Herzberg's Motivators and (mostly) Hygiene Factors. His theory, as you know, concludes that organizations do too much of the hygiene and too little of the motivator factors. The ass's dissatisfaction is literally due to negative hygiene factors as he vends his way around the "Circle of the Year in a Course of restless Labour". So, would introducing a few positives (vacations, a pail of water, sick leave, weekends off, a retirement plan) make for a more creative and happy Ass? Or, would there be only less dis-satisfaction and no real satisfaction for the Ass?

How would you address the tribulations of the "unsteady Man"?

Would you seek ways to influence the "unsettled Mind" in a co-worker or subordinate? Here's my Melanie case study, one that I use in class:

You meet Melanie for coffee everyday. Lately, Melanie is telling you she is desperate to leave her job. It'd be the first thing she would do, only if... Melanie has lots of reasons why she can't leave. You concur entirely with Melanie's desire to leave – anyone this unhappy needs to try something else. But, the only action she takes is to complain to you. Today, she tells you, "I despise this job!"

What do you advise Melanie to do? Is she not a bit like the unhappy Ass dealing with his "Drudgeries"?

Envision a scenario that makes for an improved view of life for Melanie.

How can an organization help make things better for its employees? Or, is mankind never to be free of "restless Labour"? Should we just buckle down and slog on?

Lubans

The Bee in Love

ong ago, when animals and plants could talk, a busy but weary bee landed on an especially bright yellow flower. The flower was ambrosial, enough for the bee to say to the flower; "Whoa, I want more of this!"

So, already drowsy from the day's work, he took a rest on the yellow blossom. As he snoozed the flower whispered to him and said she hoped he would stay. The bee took a deep breath – inhaling the flower's scent, wiggled his tail, and settled in where he was, his wings still, only his antenna moving now and then as he listened to the flower and they spoke of bee and flower things.

No shirker, the bee still did his daily share of work for the beehive working long hours collecting nectar. But, in the late afternoon – in a vertical free fall after a loop de loop – he'd return to his love, the yellow flower. Those first few summer's days of bliss turned into many. But, soon the days shortened, the sun hid behind rain clouds. Then, the first signs of frost soon appeared, but still the flower and the bee visited each day. And then, with a wintry wind, it ended. Whenever you see a yellow flower with a black center, think of the bee's and flower's reciprocated love.

Sometimes following one's heart is the only path.

And, so it can be at work. Instead of diligently and predictably going up the ladder, we might choose another path. Instead of pursuing proffered laurels, we stay in a job, doing what we love with little fame or fanfare but great satisfaction and personal achievement.

My Thoughts

Aesop

Aesop and the Bow*

here was an Athenian who saw Aesop shooting marbles with some boys in the street. He burst out laughing, thinking how foolish Aesop looked, an old man playing marbles — but Aesop makes fun of you; you don't make fun of Aesop. So when Aesop heard the Athenian laughing, he said nothing in reply but simply took an unstrung bow and put it down on the ground where the man could see it. Then he said, "Hey, Mr. Know-It-All, riddle me this: what does this bow mean?" Aesop's words got the people's attention, and a crowd gathered round. The Athenian was baffled; he thought and he thought, but he could not figure out the riddle, and finally he gave up. Having defeated the man in this battle of wits, Aesop then revealed the meaning of the bow. "If you have your bow tightly strung at all times, it will break. You need to let it rest sometimes so that it will be ready whenever you need it.

The human mind is like that bow: it needs to relax every once in a while.

---

* For a more literal translation, see Sources, Laura Gibbs' Oxford Aesop 537.

Even the winged Cupid has to give his bow a rest from time to time. And so it is at work. If, without cease, we keep our nose to the grindstone, our ear to the ground, our eye on the ball, and our shoulder to the wheel, we'll wind up as humorless and clichéd as the last four phrases! Worse, we'll be less productive than if we take breaks. I was surprised with the varied response from staff when I organized a "Day in the Woods". This was a playful team building experience and far away from e-mail, voice-mail, offices, desks, and computers. Some took part with enthusiasm; others were reluctant but showed up with an open mind, willing to try out something new. Others, unlike Elvis, never left the building! They saw a day off playing group games as a waste of time – or so they said. (I think the group's being a mix of supervisors and staff deterred some. From my work with corporate groups, I have seen bosses very reluctant to mix and mingle and a few appeared fearful of not doing well, of not having THE answer to a problem solving activity.)

A few even took it upon themselves to disparage others' going, and, if a subordinate wanted to go, they'd not grant permission.

Invariably, the results of those days away were new and strengthened relationships, new perspectives, and, oddly enough, fresh ideas on how to get work done. Many of my "direct reports" chose to take part; overall about 20% of the total staff volunteered.

Chapter 7

The effective leader

Aesop

Chapter 7
The effective leader
Advice giving and getting

The Fawn and his Mother

 Hind said to her Fawn, who was now well grown and strong, "My son, Nature has given you a powerful body and a stout pair of horns, and I can't think why you are such a coward as to run away from the hounds." Just then they both heard the sound of a pack in full cry, but at a considerable distance. "You stay where you are," said the Hind; "never mind me": and with that she ran off as fast as her legs could carry her.

One moralist has it that "No arguments will give courage to the coward."

Now that's a bit harsh. The deer has the statistical wisdom not to take on a pack of hounds. The odds are stacked. Still, the fable exemplifies the adage: "Do as I say, not as I do."

We are all prone to sanctimony, stating norms of behavior and then making exceptions for ourselves. So try to avoid absolutes but also avoid weasel talk. When I am obligated to read strategic plans – I normally run screaming the other way – I am struck by the language; the empty clichés, like so many helium hot dogs, pretending a robustness neither meant, understood or intended.

Lubans

Neptune and the Curlew

nce upon a time the curlew resided in Neptune's pelagic kingdom. Instead of feathers, the curlew had scales and swam in the deep ocean. While he loved the water, his curiosity took him ever toward the surface. Skimming along, he could see the sandy shore glistening under a blue sky. He dove down to tell the other fish of his adventures.

Neptune was annoyed and jealous with curlew's description of the wonders beyond the sea. He made the curlew promise not to return to the shore.

Well, as you can imagine, it was not long before the curlew once again was swimming in the rushing surf, ogling the new sights. Alas, this time he became stranded on a sandbar, a fish out of water, gasping his last. Neptune intervened and spared curlew but angry over the broken promise, changed him into a bird and banished him to the water's edge, never to return to the depths of the sea.

So, the curlew now skirts the shore and wades into the water, torn between the water and the land, plaintively calling to the unhearing sea.

Moral: Set your sights to the achievable lest you perish in the pursuit of the impossible.

Aesop

The Hawk, the Kite, and the Pigeons

he Pigeons, terrified by the appearance of a Kite, called upon the Hawk to defend them. He at once consented. When they had admitted him into the cote, they found that he made more havoc and slew a larger number of them in one day than the Kite could pounce upon in a whole year.

Avoid a remedy that is worse than the disease.

And from 1775, a moral appearing in ÆSOP'S FABLES, translated by Samuel Croxall, suggests a strong interest by revolutionary readers of Croxall's translation:

"What can this fable be applied to but the exceeding blindness and stupidity of that part of mankind who wantonly and foolishly trust their native rights of liberty without good security? …. The truth is, we ought not to incur the possibility of being deceived in so important a matter as this: an unlimited power should not be trusted in the hands of any one who is not endued with a perfection more than human."

Mr. Croxall, writing just before America's break with King George III, (over the "native rights of liberty") did not miss the point of this fable. If liberty is worth having, making concessions to "the (presumed) lesser of two evils" is to repeat the pigeons' self-destructing folly.

Today's news of a centuries-old enemy providing "free" military assistance to a hapless "former" foe and another country's "freeing" a part of a sovereign state with grand promises to those "liberated" suggest that Aesop's insights are as relevant today as they were in 550BC.

My Thoughts

Aesop

The Boy Bathing

Chapter 7
The effective leader
Less blame, more action

Boy was bathing In a river and got out of his depth, and was in great danger of being drowned. A man who was passing along a road hard by heard his cries for help, and went to the riverside and began to scold him for being so careless as to get into deep water, but made no attempt to help him. "Oh, sir," cried the Boy, "please help me first and scold me afterwards."

Give assistance, not advice, in a crisis.

One translator makes it explicit: "The fable shows that people who lecture someone during a moment of crisis are offering criticism that is inappropriate and out of place."

This epimythium (the moral at the end) is, for once, on target. When things are falling apart, don't waste time on the non-essentials like looking for causes. The drowning boy's ignorance is the obvious cause, the lesson is also obvious: Learn how to swim or avoid the water.

While it may satisfy an inner need to criticize, my asking someone "What were you thinking?" for some stupid behavior is just another form of blaming or shaming. Better to offer ideas for avoiding future failures or ask the question, "What would you be willing to do differently?"

Aesop

Jupiter, Neptune, Minerva, and Momus

ccording to an ancient legend, the first man was made by Jupiter, the first bull by Neptune, and the first house by Minerva. On the completion of their labors, a dispute arose as to which had made the most perfect work. They agreed to appoint Momus as judge, and to abide by his decision. Momus, however, being very envious of the handicraft of each, found fault with all. He first blamed the work of Neptune because he had not made the horns of the bull below his eyes, so he might better see where to strike. He then condemned the work of Jupiter, because he had not placed the heart of man on the outside, that everyone might read the thoughts of the evil disposed and take precautions against the intended mischief. And, lastly, he inveighed against Minerva because she had not contrived iron wheels in the foundation of her house, so its inhabitants might more easily remove if a neighbor proved unpleasant. Jupiter, indignant at such inveterate faultfinding, drove him from his office of judge, and expelled him from the mansions of Olympus.

Since being cast out of Olympus, Momus has lightened up. Less humorless carping, more humor. So, today he is more about mockery. Each Mardi Gras, New Orleans' Knights of Momus krewe again engage in the revelry now associated with their namesake.

So, if you must nitpick, find fault, your message with go further with a dose of levity. Or, forget finding fault; focus on improvement and change rather than on what's wrong.

In the workplace, nitpicking and faultfinding is institutionalized in something called Performance Appraisal. Promoted – with no evidence – as a formal process for employee improvement it has gained a well deserved notoriety as the most hated piece of management work: assigning a numerical value to another human being.

Wm. Deming had this to say about the effect of formal performance appraisal: "... It leaves people bitter, crushed, bruised, battered, desolate. despondent, dejected, feeling inferior, some even depressed, unfit for work for weeks after receipt of a rating, unable to comprehend why they are inferior."

Hyperbole? You decide.

My Thoughts

Aesop

The Jar Who Went to Court*

here was a woman from the ancient Greek city of Sybaris who broke a jar. The jar decided to take the woman to court, summoning witnesses to testify against her. The woman exclaimed, "What a foolish jar you are! You don't need a judge and jury; you need a plaster bandage to hold yourself together!"

How often do we waste time in getting even, in pointing out other's mistakes, when we should instead just pick up the pieces and start over? Instead of proclaiming you've been wronged, take action that moves you further along. If something is broken, forget fixing blame; rather fix what's broken!

PS. Often what's not broken needs to be broken, but that's another fable.

* For a more literal translation, see in Sources, Laura Gibbs' Oxford Aesop 180.

Aesop

The Shipwrecked Man

 rich Athenian was sailing with some other travelers. A violent tempest suddenly arose, and the boat capsized. Then, while the other passengers were trying to save themselves by swimming, the Athenian continually invoked the aid of the goddess Athena and promised offering after offering if only she would save him.

One of his shipwrecked companions, who swam beside him, said to him: 'Appeal to Athena by all means, but also move your arms!'

I can apply the lesson to myself; but economically hapless Greece et al., first come to mind.

Self-management is one of the concepts I stress in my Democratic Workplace class.

"Self-management" deals with becoming an effective follower, someone who stands out because she is pro-active and thinks critically for herself; she is more leader-like than waiting-to-be-led. An effective follower has a good idea of who he is and is not afraid to speak the truth. She has a strong professional purpose and values to match.

Barbara Kellerman's book, Bad Leadership, offers advice on what followers can do when working with a bad leader. That same advice helps define self-management:

Empower yourself.

Be loyal to the whole, not to any one individual.

Be skeptical.

Take a stand.

Pay attention.

These concepts may be difficult to instill – if you are not already inclined that way from experience or gene pool – but I still think a person can evolve and gain more knowledge about who he is.

Experience helps us acquire lessons, to find courage for the "next time". If we regret our performance in one situation, how will we do better the next time? If we backed down from an abusive boss or if we were abusive to someone, what will we change about the next time?

My Thoughts

Abstemius

An Eele and a Snake

Chapter 7
The effective leader
More humor, please

ou and I are so alike, says the Eele to the Snake, that methinks we should be somewhat a-kin; and yet they that persecute me, are afraid of you. What should be the reason of this? Oh (says the Snake) because no body does me an Injury but I make him smart for't.

In all Controversies they come off best that keep their Adversaries in fear of a Revenge.

So, bite your tongue or bite the attackers head off? Abstemius suggests that the fear – not necessarily action – of "a Revenge" is what keeps the adversary at bay. Snarling like a junkyard dog will get you labeled as uptight, thin-skinned, paranoid, and, horrors, un-cool!

In the workplace we're told to turn away, that karma will come around and bite the maligner. Eventually.

Instead, cultivate humor as your vehicle of revenge, the snake's stinging bite; petty people abhor ridicule.

Aesop

The Dog and the Reeds*

eware the company you keep. There was once a dog who liked to poop in the reeds by the river. The reeds didn't like this at all, so one of them poked the dog in the butt. The dog jumped back and began to bark at the reeds, but the reed replied, 'Bark all you want! I'd rather listen to you complain at a distance than have to smell your dirty business nearby.'

What to do when someone dumps on you? When disparaged, does one exhibit umbrage (whatever that is) or sit in dignified silence. I suppose it depends; as the fable declares, even the reed has a limit.

There are some circumstances (like the reed's) that justify jabbing back, getting some distance. The difficulty is in knowing how to respond, when to roar and when to purr. A respected friend advised me, early in my career, it was best not to respond to the "slings and arrows of outrageous fortune". A true gentleman, he firmly believed and practiced that reacting to a slur or slander only would lend dignity to the pejorative comment. Ignore it and it will go away. For me, turning the other cheek worked most of the time but not always.

* For a more literal translation, see in Sources, Laura Gibbs' Oxford Aesop 566.

It's probably best to respond to the perceived insult with something comical; humor is better than the risk of looking foolish through angry over-reaction or appearing a milquetoast. So, ramp up your repartee. However, "Yo Momma" does not qualify as a snappy comeback!

My Thoughts

Lubans

The Kudzu Vine and the Oak Tree

Chapter 7
The effective leader
Don't forget your roots

 long time ago the kudzu creeper and an oak tree were neighbors. Not very good neighbors, because the oak tree daily reminded the kudzu of its lowly status and of the oak's lofty importance. Disdainfully, the oak showered the kudzu with its old leaves, acorns and other droppings. Finally the kudzu appealed to Zeus for relief. Zeus granted the kudzu's wish to climb; no longer would it be earth bound. Soon the kudzu vine crept up the trunk of the oak tree, along its branches and it was not long before it engulfed the tree. The kudzu smothered the sunlight and sapped water from the tree. The oak died and the kudzu, high above the earth and no longer humble, exulted. It was now as prideful as ever had been the oak.

But not for long. The dead oak's branches sagged and its roots withered. Zeus sent a harsh wind, toppling the tree and the kudzu crashed back to earth, unseemly ambition and pride its undoing.

And so it can be in the workplace when a "good" subordinate is chosen to replace a bad leader. The proud new leader may soon forget all her good intentions and become even a worse leader.

My Thoughts

Sources

Aesop, and Laura Gibbs. 2002. Aesop's fables. Oxford: Oxford University Press.

Her "Aesopica : Aesop's fables in English, Latin and Greek" at http://mythfolklore.net/aesopica/index.htm is the gateway to rich troves of fable literature.

Aesop, and Milo Winter. 1919. The Æsop for Children. With pictures by Milo Winter. Rand, McNally & Co: Chicago.

Aesop, Roger L'Estrange, and Stephen Gooden. 1992. Fables. (Everyman's Library Children's Classics) New York: Knopf.

Aesop, Walter Crane, and W. J. Linton. 1887. The Baby's Own Æsop: being the Fables condensed in rhyme [by W.J. Linton], with portable morals pictorially painted by Walter Crane, etc. G. London & New York: Routledge & Sons.

Aesopus, V.S. Vernon Jones, Gilbert Keith Chesterton, and Arthur Rackham. 1975. Fables: a new translation. London: Pan.

Ésope, and Roger L'Estrange. 1692. Fables of Aesop and other eminent mythologists [Barlandus, Anianus, Abstemius, Poggius], with morals and reflexions, by sir Roger L'Estrange. London: R. Sare.

Greenaway, John, George Fyler Townsend, and Harrison Weir. 1882. Three hundred and fifty Aesop's fables. Chicago: Belford, Clarke & Co.

Group 3: Viktorija Vaitkune; Zane Zvaigzne, Gita Ruševica; Elita Vīksna; Agnese Kokneviča; Liene Kalneta; Eva Ausēja.
Group 5: Evita Stankeviča; Lana Augule; Inga Vovčenko; Tamāra Černišova; Ilona Vēliņa-Švilpe; Ieva Krūmiņa; Viktorija Moskina.
Their fables (Cat and Mouse & The Fox Gets Left Behind) were written at the "Wisdom in a Thimble: Managers and Fables" discussion led by John Lubans at the National Library of Latvia in Riga, February 24, 2016.

La Fontaine, Jean de. 1841. Fables of La Fontaine. Translated from the French by Elizur Wright, Jr . Boston: Published by Elizur Wright, Jr. and Tappan and Dennet.

Larned, W. T., Jean de La Fontaine, and John Rae. 1918. Fables in rhyme for little folks: adapted from the French of La Fontaine. New York: P.F. Volland.

Lubans, John. 2010. Leading from the middle, and other contrarian essays on library leadership. Santa Barbara, California: Libraries Unlimited/ABC-CLIO.

Lubans, John. 2010 – "Leading from the Middle".
http://blog.lubans.org
  Published since late 2010, this blog supplements the book, Leading from the Middle. Twice weekly postings, including a "Friday Fable", the source for "Fables for Leaders".

Odo, and John C. Jacobs. 1985. The fables of Odo of Cheriton. Syracuse, New York: Syracuse University Press.

Strachey, Lionel. 1905. The world's wit and humor; an encyclopedia of the classic wit and humor of all ages and nations. New York: The Review of Reviews Co.

Thornbury, Walter, and Gustave Doré. 1900. The fables of Lafontaine. New York: Cassell & Company.

Wodehouse, P. G. 1935. Blandings castle. Pp. 218-240. Garden City, New York: Doubleday, Doran.

Fabulists

Abstemius, Laurentius c.1440-1508

The professor Laura Gibbs offers these biographical details:

"Lorenzo Bevilaqua (his family name) was a fifteenth-century Italian scholar. Although he was the author of various scholarly works, he was best known for his Hecatomythium Secundum, a collection of 100 'original' Aesop's fables inspired by the classical tradition of Aesop's fables, (Venice, 1499) It is a truly marvelous collection of fables, marked by sharp social satire, including satire directed against the church. Aesop himself would definitely approve!

Abstemius was librarian to Duke Guido Ubaldo under Pope Alexander VI."

Aesop, c.620-c.560 BCE

"The life of Aesop is a bit of a mystery" starts out one biographical attempt. Indeed! Was Aesop a pseudonym? Was he a slave? Was he a mute to whom speech was given as a divine gift? Did he have physical disabilities? Was he of African descent? Did his sharp tongue – or was it thievery – lead to his being hurled off of a cliff in Delphi to his death?

And so it goes.

Myth or not, he is mentioned in Greek history, particularly by the Greek historian Herodotus and Aristotle. Plutarch put Aesop at the court of Croesus, the king of Lydia (Turkey). Another contemporary source from Egypt describes Aesop as a slave from Samos, an island near Turkey.

Aesop has also been referred to as a Phrygian, suggesting another link to Turkey.

One source has it that, "the name 'Aesop' is a variant of 'Acthiop,' which is "Ethiopia" in ancient Greek. "This and the trickster nature of some of his stories, where humans are regularly outwitted by a cleverer animal figure, has led some scholars to speculate that Aesop may have been from Africa."

In any case, Aesop is credited with more than six hundred oral fables and with inspiring countless other storytellers and fabulists, old and new. And, unquestionably, his brilliantly pithy stories have delighting and instructed young and old readers of every century.

The first extant version of the fables is thought to be from Phaedrus, a former slave from Macedonia who translated the tales into Latin in the first century. Aesop's tales were known in medieval Europe, and Caxton translated a German edition he brought back to England (from Germany) along with a printing press, the first in England. Caxton's Aesop was one of the first books printed in English.

Ivan Krylov 1769–1844

A Russian fabulist, playwright, and journalist was born in Moscow and educated at home. He often provoked the wrath of the Russian government with his satirical compositions, yet was neither imprisoned nor banished.

He achieved literary fame in the 1790s. Possibly due to his reputed laziness, he gave up writing for a decade. In any case, he was, and is, a popular – indeed beloved – literary figure in Russia.

One of his sinecures was that of Librarian of the Imperial Public Library (from 1816).

L'Estrange, Sir Roger 1616-1704

According to the Britannica, he was one of the earliest of English journalists and pamphleteers and an ardent support-er of the Royalist cause during the English Civil Wars and Commonwealth period (1649–60).

After an unsuccessful skirmish against anti-Royalist forc-es in 1644, he was imprisoned for four years.

He published three newssheets: the Intelligencer, the News and the Observator. Due to his zealous rooting out of sedition he earned the nickname "Bloodhound of the Press". He was knighted in 1685. After King James II lost the throne, L'Estrange was forced to retire. A linguist, he supported his wife and himself chiefly by translations of many standard authors, including in 1692, according to Laura Gibbs, "what is still the single greatest compilation of Aesop's fables in English, a mighty volume entitled 'Fables of Aesop ...'".

Professor Gibbs concludes: "... L'Estrange ranks as one of the most lively masters of prose in 17th-century Eng-land, and his hyperbolic, racy style is quite astounding. I wish our political discourse today were as witty and well written!"

La Fontaine: Jean de 1621-1695

A great French writer Jean de La Fontaine wrote his first original work – the small epic "Adonis"- in 1658. Dedicated to the soon to be disgraced Fouquet, La Fontaine fled to Limoges to avoid the ire of Louis the 14th.

From 1664 to 1672, he was housed by a patron in the Palais du Luxembourg. Here, Fontaine wrote his main work, the fables. Appearing in 1668 as "Fables choisies, mises en vers" in two volumes. La Fontaine had difficulties with increasing censorship and the banning of at least one of his books. Still, in 1683, La Fontaine was appointed to the Académie Française.

Lubans, John 1941-

After an adventurous career in academic administration, Lubans is now a somewhat retired librarian. He has held leadership roles in several public and private universities and taught internationally.

Currently, as a visiting professor at the University of Latvia, he teaches about freedom at work and democratic workplaces.

Early in his career, as a research interest, he authored and edited the book, "Educating the Library User" which anticipated and promoted the development of many programs for information literacy.

As an English major, he regularly uses literary allusions in his writing and teaching, e.g. drawing from Cervantes, PG Wodehouse, Timma Mirzda and James Thurber.

In 2010, he published "Leading from the Middle and Other Contrarian Essays on Library Leadership." Concurrent with the book, he began his eponymous twice-weekly blog on leadership, teamwork and democratic workplaces along with the weekly Friday Fables from which this book derives.

He was an independent Fulbright Scholar in 2011 and 2014.

Odo of Cheriton c.1185–c.1246

English preacher and fabulist, his best-known work is a collection of moralized fables and anecdotes in Latin. "Though partly composed of commonly known adaptations and extracts, it shows originality and the moralizations are full of pungent denunciations of the prevalent vices of clergy and laity."

Some seventy-five fables in number, twenty-six of them come from the Aesop corpus. No doubt inspired by Aesopic traditions, Odo created other fables taken from stories by Roman writers, from medieval writers and from the Bible and English folktales.

Laura Gibbs: "Odo's Latin fables were well known and circulated widely, as evidenced by numerous manuscript copies as well as translations into Spanish, French, and Welsh. Odo was a very learned man for his time, having studied in the schools of Paris, but he was not a high-brow scholar. Instead, he intended for his writings to appeal to a general audience, embracing both the clergy and lay people. Many of the fables evince a strong sympathy for the poor and oppressed, with often sharp criticisms of high-ranking church officials."

Editor: **Sheryl Anspaugh**

Illustrations: **Béatrice Coron**

Illuminated letters: **William Morris (1834-1896)**

Design: **Alise Šnēbaha**

Software: Adobe InDesign, Adobe Illustrator
Typefaces: Lucida Fax, Plantagenet Cherokee, Post Antiqua

EZIS PRESS